Just Go In

To everyone I've learned from,
especially my children.

ACKNOWLEDGEMENTS

To my Mother, Sisters and Brother – intelligent, brave and decent people who all deserved a lighter load. My cousin Lynn and her family.

With love to:

Dmytro Morykit, for his love and support and his music which carries me forward. My children, Robin Whytock, who kindly spent precious time in the wee small hours, editing large chunks; Rory Whytock, for support and understanding, and Heather Cameron Whytock, for patience and endless prodding and my two grandchildren, Jason and Rowan for making everything bright.

My gratitude to:

Gonzalo Mazzei, for encouragement in publishing this book and Margaret Bennett for the introduction.

Patricia Ace and Lilla Scott, my *Lippy Bissom* friends, who support and enrich my writing and personal life.

Janice Campbell, for the friendship.

Tessa Ransford, for being an inspiration and making profound connections.

Rachel Fox and Elizabeth Gibbs, for reading an early draft and gifting helpful suggestions and edits.

So many others have helped in different ways; mostly they've been unaware of doing so.

Acknowledgement also goes to the *Scottish Book Trust* and *BBC Radio Scotland* for publishing and broadcasting the chapter, *A toe in the line*, selected by Hardeep Singh Kohli, for the 'Days Like This' project (2008).

CONTENTS

*It is queer how it is always one's virtues
and not one's vices that precipitate
one into disaster.*
Rebecca West

1

Hidden tracks

The air felt damp but the ground was dry as I lay trying not to move in case they might sense my presence. It was almost midsummer, the lush leaves and grasses provided excellent cover and although I was a little uncomfortable, I was frightened to move in the slightest. I thought it must be nearly 8 o'clock, almost time for their appearance. I'd been lying here for almost an hour. I liked to arrive early in case they changed their time but they never did, they arrived at exactly the same time each night. I thought of home: an upstairs flat on a run-down council estate, not a very large estate, small enough for everyone to know each other. The houses themselves were not so bad, with big airy rooms and large gardens, but many had been left to deteriorate both inside and out; the bathrooms were old and chipped, the windows were rotting and draughty and the harling was in desperate need of repair. It was a typical grey Scottish council estate. However, an odd thing had recently happened, the council had decided to tidy it up from the outside and had begun repairing the harling then painting it bizarre colours. The first house was yellow, then the next one pink, it was a valiant attempt to cheer up the standard dirty-white blocks of houses, but this was not a sunny resort, it was a dreich, wet, West of Scotland, where houses were built as barriers to the elements. The original architects had not thought about the appearance; there was no suitably attractive local stone or distinctive slate and tiles, even the privately built houses were clones of each other, these housing estates were built for practicality and at the least cost. On the plus side, they'd all been given decent sized gardens and it was here that you found the colour and creativity of people who had long ago lost the fight but were still battling on, no longer sure who the enemy was any more, just that there was one.

Some of the gardens were unkempt and overgrown, most had a geometrical tidiness and several cascaded in colour and greenery beyond their own expectations. These usually belonged to elderly residents, who took a pride in everything, whilst keeping themselves to themselves. The roads were quiet as not many of the residents owned cars. Possession of a car, no matter what condition, put the owners on pedestals of success; a sign they might be going somewhere.

I was the second of five children. My mother would be sitting with a cup of tea before doing a bit of housework, then settling down for the evening to watch TV or do a crossword. I glanced at the binoculars beside me - I would need them soon. My father would be in his other home - the local pub. I knew he wouldn't be back till late, it was a Friday evening - pay day. I wondered if there would be any money left for Mum this week; there were many weeks when there was no money from him. He had heard of a great tip for a horse or greyhound and put everything on it - *it* being a certainty until it was inevitably second, third or still standing. If he ever actually won, then it was no consolation, as he would immediately put the winnings on the next certainty, convinced that one day he would win so much money that he could make everyone happy. He'd dress Mum in beautiful clothes, my sister would get her dreamed-of horse and me, well, he couldn't make much of me though he did buy the binoculars - or so I thought.

Suddenly there was movement, I held my breath and tried to remain still, I didn't want them to know I was watching. Did they realise I was here? I remained motionless. Their small noses twitched and sniffed the air, and then a few more rabbits appeared from behind a small hillock, I knew then they were not aware of me, or perhaps they knew I meant them no harm. I liked to think they knew that. One leapt in the air, quickly followed by another, suddenly the field became a terrific playground and I too was alive. I lifted the binoculars to bring them closer, their noses twitching cutely, their soft gentle faces almost smiling, their delight in life made me delight in mine. This was heaven; only a short walk from my house, through a grass field and behind the big stone walls of the Currying Shop which seemed to belong there more than the trees themselves. This was a paradise apparently unnoticed by those who lived so near. Some locals used it as a shortcut to the next village. I would occasionally see them hurrying along the muddy, narrow path, few would take time to stop and look at what surrounded them. I was 11 years old when I first came to the Lade; it became my salvation through my growing years.

As the light faded and the dampness of the air penetrated the ground beneath me, I rolled from under the bramble branches, pulled up my duffle coat hood to cover my head and slowly wandered back home - happy.

* * * *

I sat with my career teacher for some time as she flicked through her book making various suggestions, Hotel Management, Banking, Teaching, the list went on. At the previous week's career convention, I'd sought out a small man in a dark suit to find out how I could become a journalist. It's impossible to get into journalism, he said, as though he couldn't understand why I would even consider such a career. I sat in silence with my mother beside me, she tried to quiz him further and he made a few suggestions, but I was too busy absorbing the impact of the revelation and wondering what I would do now. My other rather obscure career option was to work for the Forestry Commission, but I was told I'd have to go to university and believed that was something other people did, not people like me. The very concept was alien, and although I was at a highly regarded grammar school where many pupils went on to university, I was aware that I was there by accident rather than ability. I'd attended the local comprehensive for the first two years of my secondary education, and as was customary in the 1970s, we sat an exam aimed at creaming off the high achievers to move them to grammar schools. I'd always harboured a wish to go to Paisley Grammar, it was on the main bus route to Glasgow and I would stare at it from the bus windows imagining I belonged in the distinguished red stone building with its impressive towers and entrance gates; making it look like a school from an Enid Blyton novel. My elder sister had passed the exam and been offered a place but she turned it down because she was shy, wary of change and her best friend had not been offered the opportunity to move. I tried to persuade her to take it up, but by then she was set on a career with horses and saw little point in putting herself through the stress of moving school when she intended to leave as soon as she turned 16.

The next year, my friend Fay and I sat in the main hall to hear the selected list of pupils names read out by the Headmaster, Mr Hamilton. We listened eagerly as he read through the list; Fay especially hoped to be named as her brother had gone to John Neilson, the other option to the Grammar. The Head finished the list but neither Fay nor I were included and Fay was very disappointed, and though I felt disappointment, I was unsurprised. Then, as the Headmaster stood to leave, he turned and said, 'anyone who was not mentioned but feels they should be considered, please come and see me in my office after the break'. Fay was desperate to go and ask him to reconsider. We discussed the pro's and con's of doing so with my sister and her friend in the playground - I didn't see the point of going but eventually agreed to give moral support to Fay, I had no intention of asking him to reconsider me, one disappointment had been enough.

We knocked and entered the Headmaster's room, it was a small room and he sat behind a cluttered desk, I managed to creep around the door and stuck fast to it as Fay went forward - she explained why she was keen to go to John Neilson as her brother was there. He looked out her records, studied them for a few minutes, made some comments and asked her a few questions. Then said he would not recommend her to be moved as he thought she could not cope with the work, I was disappointed for her but hadn't really expected anything different; I felt sure his mind was already made up. I turned to open the door then heard him ask for my name, I gave it but mumbled something about not questioning his decision - he ignored this and flicked through the paperwork. 'You have good exam results in everything but Maths - why?' I was flattered and grabbed at the first excuse which came to mind; I had been ill a lot (I had asthma and was ill quite often) but the real reason was I hated Maths and the Maths teacher and would often skip class. It was easy to skip classes, no one ever noticed and we would go off to the shopping centre or over the other side of the bing and hang about until something more interesting was on the timetable. There was silence as he sat looking at the papers. I couldn't believe my ears when he said he would consider me for a move and handed me a form to take home to my parents. I was stunned but couldn't show too much pleasure as I knew how badly Fay felt. She was going to get her Dad to write a letter. Meanwhile, I desperately suppressed my delight and the need to run around exclaiming that I had a form to complete. My mother was delighted with the news, and on returning the form I was allocated a place at the Grammar.

I loved my two years at Paisley Grammar, I worried before starting that I might not fit in as I didn't speak 'properly', so I'd rehearse speaking better English as I lay in bed at night. It therefore came as a shock when I discovered that I was not at all out of place. However, soon after starting, I quickly realised that the Headmaster had misread my exam results in French. I'd been placed in the top class. On the first day of French, I was asked to read out some basic grammar. I sat turning bright red and staring at the book in front of me. 'Je suis…'. I stuttered, as the teacher became infuriated at me, until she finally realised I hadn't a clue. She asked me to remain behind after class. I stood beside her desk as she took out notes on the new entrants, ran her finger down to my name and queried why I couldn't answer a simple question when I'd obtained an 83% in my entrance exam? I had to tell her the figure was wrong and I'd only achieved 33%. Surprisingly, she didn't have me thrown out of her class or returned to the comprehensive as I feared but persevered with me. I rewarded her when I achieved an 'O' level in the subject, much to her delight and relief. So, it was all a fluke, but a fluke that would have a huge impact on my life.

2

Rabbit boxes and cow licks

I could tell by my career teacher's voice that she was becoming frustrated at my lack of interest in her suggestions then she flicked past 'Farm Secretary'. I put my hand out and said 'Wait'. She turned the page and began reading the notes. My attachment to the countryside was so strong that anything to do with it sounded ideal. My career teacher wasn't so keen, I had eight high grade 'O' levels and three Highers, the requirements for the Farm Secretary course was only three 'O' levels. 'It would be such a waste of your ability'. She said. However, I wanted to choose a job that I would enjoy, after all, my father had told me I would be spending most of my life working, I may as well enjoy what I did. He was a tanner, but with no qualifications there was little chance for him to change. He hated his work and spent every Monday looking forward to Friday. I didn't want to do that.

I headed straight to the school library where I found a book about Farm Secretaries, but I didn't read it, the cover was enough to convince me it would be the career I imagined: a girl standing in a byre with her wellies on, notebook in hand, surrounded by friendly cows and a cheery farmer - the only thing missing was a bit of straw in his mouth. The next day I informed my mother and career teacher of my decision to become a Farm Secretary and a letter was sent to the only college in Scotland that provided the necessary qualification. My father couldn't see the point of going to college but Mum encouraged me and she only became more determined as my father began to complain about the cost. The college was at the other side of Scotland, which to me was the other side of the world. I'd heard about it, and once on a holiday I'd met people from there, so I knew they spoke differently, using strange words like 'ken', but I'd never been there myself. I imagined it to be some kind of exotic paradise and even visited a local travel agent to obtain brochures. The brochures confirmed my ideas: filled with pictures of lochs, fishing, gliding and even skiing, adding to the attraction. The six-mile bus journey between home and school had now worn off; it was time to expand my horizons.

Fifteen years on, I stood in the middle of the sunny agricultural showground with my two children watching interestingly. An explanation was being given by a farmer on how the rabbit box worked; '...

they run over it for several days, then you loosen the catch and the next time they run over the hatch opens and they drop into the box below. They can then be removed at the end of the day and destroyed'. Yes, I knew a rabbit was a creature of habit, didn't I? Here I was looking at rabbits from a different perspective: that of the farmer, gardener, and forester. They saw them as a pest, only vermin. My mind slid back to those happy evenings and the day I discovered a copper snare placed close to 'my rabbits' homes. I felt disgusted as I wrenched it from the ground, running through the long, wet grass finding more, pulling them up in horror and wondering why someone would want to kill these beautiful creatures. I was equally horrified that someone else had been walking around my special place. I looked around the showground and considered the new knowledge that had altered my perspective and how much had changed since the days when I would have done anything to protect these creatures.

My love of the countryside did little to reduce my ignorance of it; I walked for several miles along the Lade, winter was now over and a new life was returning to everything around me. Buds appeared everywhere I looked. There was still a chill in the air but the sky was blue and bright. Instead of remaining on the path, I decided on a new route and climbed the wooden gate into a ploughed field. As I began to cross the field I noticed a potato lying beside the ploughed ridge. Its skin was red and as I bent to lift it I noticed another just under the earth, I pulled it out and realised the whole field was full of potatoes - what a remarkable find. We rarely ate potatoes now as they were too expensive; I would take some home for dinner. I walked through the muddy, bumpy field as if I was walking through a field of gold. It seemed such a crime that the farmer had just left them there. Lifting the small red potatoes, I filled my duffle coat pockets and then its hood. I walked home weighed down by a coat full of potatoes excited by how pleased my mother would be. On arrival home I emptied my pockets onto the kitchen table and my mother surprised but pleased lifted one and said "These are my favourite. Where did you get them?" when I told her of my new found treasure I was disappointed to be told they would have just been planted and I shouldn't have lifted them. I had presumed potatoes were grown from seeds, but what a treat we had for dinner that evening.

When I began college I was only 16 and had obtained 'digs' in a local household, a pleasant family with a modern bungalow, and although privately owned it was similar to most Scottish housing, that is, it was almost exactly the same as all other houses in the vicinity. The place reminded me of my school friend Catherine's house; precise and neat inside, everything seemed to belong and have a place - there were no 'extras' anywhere. I thought of them as shiny houses, as everything seemed to sparkle. My Mum would have loved such a house; she'd once been given the chance to buy a house in Bridge of Weir for £500. A friend was moving and offered it to my Mum before putting it on the market, but Dad was against it, he thought the extra costs involved would be too much. Instead Mum made the most of the council house, decorating with creativity: I helped her paint the hallway with leftover pots of paint. She painted each strip of wallpaper a different colour and then covered the divide with thin coloured tape. It was cheerful and effective. When I was twelve, we had to move house because we needed an extra room. I didn't like it as much as our first house which had a large garden filled with rowan trees. This one was a flat above another house, although it did have a good sized garden, there were no trees. I'd helped Mum with the moving, including a piano which none of us could play but I loved having. We wheeled it down the bumpy road between houses and it jangled sounds of shock and frustration the entire way. It was a difficult job getting it up the stairs, but we tied ropes and between us, managed to haul it up. The carpets were too big, so Mum rolled out the living room carpet on the lawn and that evening, by the moonlight, she laid the carpet from the house on top and cut around it with a Stanley knife. It then fitted perfectly.

My Landlords had two children, a teenage boy and a slightly younger girl; to me this was a fairy tale life, the picture book family. There was no drunken father, hand-me-down clothes or a house void of food. I was struck by the husband and wife relationship, he would always speak politely and call her 'dear', he was even nice to her when I thought he shouldn't be. He helped a lot in the house, cooked dinner, washed dishes and showed interest in his children's school work without being asked. As they laughed together one day I knew this was the kind of relationship I wanted. However, as the weeks passed I soon realised that not everything was as it first appeared and there is always a price to pay, the unspoken compromises.

Because I was just 16, the couple thought I was too young to be away from home and family. It was as though they were trying to be surrogate parents: Always asking where I was going in the evenings and who I was with. I was not used to being fussed over, my mother having had five children and a husband who would occasionally hand over £10 at the end of the week, had eventually gone to work when I was ten. Mum was not looking for a career, she needed the money - often there would be no gas or electricity in the house, we had gas and electric meters but my dad would pick the locks and help himself to the contents. This was something he taught me; how to pick a lock. I thought of it as a necessary skill that everyone learned, but one day when the insurance man called, he couldn't open the lock on his briefcase and was very flustered when he realised he'd lost the key. I was twelve and innocently said, 'don't worry, my dad has shown me how to open locks without a key, I can do it with a Kirby Grip'. The look on my mother's face was enough to make me realise I'd said something terrible: she stood up and pushed me out of the room, 'Don't be silly Hazel - that was just for your school bag'. I knew not to argue. However, it was something that came in handy several times over the years, much to the surprise of those I helped. There were times when Mum hadn't managed to replace the money before the meter man called and we had to hide behind the sofa or in our bedrooms and stay very quiet to pretend there was no one in. We used gas for cooking but on one occasion when there was no money for the meter and only eggs in the house, mum fried them on the base of the iron. It cooked the eggs perfectly but she needed a new iron by the time she was finished as it overheated and blew up before the last egg had cooked. Mum had a practical way about her; never making a fuss about these things, just dealing with whatever was thrown at her. As a child everything is normal, it's not until we grow that we discover others live different lives.

Mum waited until we were all at school before applying for a job, she had no problem finding work, not just because she was intelligent - she was, but she also had an attractive personality. Soon Mum began to train as a Manageress for Ladbrokes and very soon she was in charge of her own shop. Mum enjoyed her job but the hours were long and she would never arrive home before 7pm. We therefore had to see to ourselves after school. A well-intentioned neighbour must have reported us to the Social Work Department as one day just after we arrived home; a very smart lady appeared at our door asking to speak to our parents. My big sister had answered the door and I stood behind taking careful notice. Even at that age we knew something was not right about this lady and we became defensive. 'Our Mum is working and Dad has just gone out for a short while'. We lied. She invited herself into the house by walking past us and asked to have a look around 'Who cooks your dinner?' she quizzed, as she wandered into the kitchen, eyes searching across the table top, sink, cupboards - I immediately responded, 'my Dad does'. I met my sister's eyes and we both knew to be careful. Luckily there was no food to cook, so we weren't being caught on that one and the kitchen was spotless. I didn't like her, she spoke to us as if we didn't understand what she was asking, but I understood she was not there to help. She walked up the stairs and we followed: she had the air of superiority - my mother also had an air of superiority but one that came from a quiet knowledge and kindness, whereas this woman we sensed was anything but kind. Suddenly she gasped and stepped backwards – we looked at her in amazement – why would anyone be frightened of kittens? Our cat was lying on a towel, laid on the floor of the bedroom cupboard nursing her new born kittens. The woman pulled out a notepad and started scribbling; we stared, daring her to move them. Eventually she left and that was the end of things as far as we were concerned. I have no idea what happened about the visit as Mum never mentioned it to us, other than to say that council tenants are not supposed to keep pets. However, I do know that Mum and Dad argued that night. This is why we became independent from an early age and although we were blessed with a lot of luck in surviving the fights between ourselves and the many other hazards, we learned to look after ourselves well.

So at sixteen, I found it difficult to have people fret over me. Mrs D. worried about me travelling alone, I was puzzled; why would anyone be concerned about me going on a train by myself? I could see no hazard in this. This complete lack of understanding on both our parts created tensions. Mrs D. must have felt a responsibility towards me but it was something I could not comprehend.

I loved college: met lots of new and interesting people, my friend who shared the 'digs' with me was from a wealthy farming family and had gone to St Leonard's, an all-girls boarding school. She thought I was rather funny and very naive; she tried to educate me on the subject of men, something she seemed to know a lot about despite having gone to an all-girls school. Kissing is fun she would say as I recounted my only experience being awful. She explained the delights of 'French kissing' - it did sound interesting. Wendy thought we should find some men to practice on. We didn't have to wait long; the next weekend there was a disco being held in a nearby village hall and a group of us piled into a Citroen Diane belonging to one of the better-off members of the class. This car was affectionately named the 'puddle jumper'. We hurtled along with great enthusiasm and much giggling. It wasn't long before we were dancing with two suitably attractive friends and I was most impressed at Wendy's ability to quickly procure a ride home for us in their car. As we pulled up to the digs, they drove around the corner from the house and parked in the darkest corner of the crescent. I was sitting in the front with my guy and Wendy was in the back. I didn't turn around when we stopped as there had been enough subtle noises emanating from the rear seats to ensure I kept looking ahead. Before I knew it, I was pulled across the seat and was being kissed, and kissed, and so it went on, until my lips and my neck began to ache and I understood that kissing, French, English or any variation was not going to be for me. Eventually, I gave in and spoke to Wendy 'I think we should go in'. She immediately opened the door, then waved goodbye and headed towards the house, telephone numbers in hand. 'What the heck took you so long?' she said, 'I thought you were going to be there all night!' 'Bloody hell', I replied, 'I was waiting on you'. We giggled our way up the dark stairs. We were so different and yet there was much common ground between us. It gave me confidence to have such a cool and able friend around.

I had never considered myself a 'townie' but soon realised I knew very little about farming and the countryside; like the majority of people, my views were rather romantic and based on myths rather than fact. Now being in a class composed of mainly farmer's daughters, I was suddenly very much a townie. However, this did not diminish my enthusiasm and if I didn't know I just asked - this strategy often created great hilarity amongst my fellow classmates. On our first visit to the college farm, we walked along the fields as the lecturer spoke at great length about the stocking policy; one word kept recurring which I had never heard before, so I asked 'what kind of animal is a heifer?' I thought I was hearing about a new species. My kindly lecturer managed to explain without laughter that it is a young female cow that hadn't had a calf yet, but the rest of the class found my lack of knowledge hilarious. I soon discovered that some heifers have a tough time in becoming cows: We had to help the vet with a difficult calving; ropes were tied around two tiny feet dangling from the back end of a heifer lying on the straw and roaring rather disturbingly. Several of us were instructed to hold the ropes and help the vet pull the calf out; this turned out to be no easy task and one that required more of a tug of war team than a group of Farm Secretaries. After several attempts, the calf emerged and we moved out of the way. I asked the next day if all had turned out OK and was reassured that the heifer and calf were doing fine. However, it didn't help in making childbirth something to look forward to.

My only other encounter with a cow was in the college byre. Notebook in hand, I walked through the muddy byre and edged my way up beside the cow to mark down its food rations, which were chalked on a little blackboard at the top of its pen. Without provocation, the cow swung its body towards me and pinned me firmly against the concrete partition. I made several attempts to push it away before eventually calling for help. Several of my classmates came to my rescue, they slapped, pushed and pulled at the beast, yanking harshly on its tail, but with the greatest of ease the more they pulled the tighter it pinned me to the wall. It was time to recruit the help of a man but then, quite suddenly, to my great relief the cow took a slow look round, stepped to the side, and I was free. There were to be no more close encounters with these beasts as far as I was concerned.

We visited the college farm weekly and I loved being there, even though I was remorselessly teased about the never-ending farming jargon I didn't understand. On one of those lovely sunny days that make you feel there is no better place to be. We stood at the top of a softly, sloping hill discussing the finer details of grass mixtures. The male lecturer, who obviously enjoyed the company of his fifteen absorbed female students spoke freely and enthusiastically. We were dressed as usual in our jeans and woolly jumpers, our hair was blowing lightly in the warm wind. Although the hill was not very high, it gave a panoramic view across much of the college farm and surrounding countryside. We looked down towards a field of sheep and the lecturer, who was holding a large sack throughout his deliberations, said 'Who wants to go to the field over there and feed the sheep?' He held up the bag of feed and I jumped at the chance. Enthused by my success at being chosen, I took the bag of feed and bounced down the field, over a gate and into the next field where the lovely, fluffy sheep were some distance away. I walked over to the long, narrow wooden troughs, lying tipped over and I carefully righted them. Then, as I raised the bag of feed, a mass of sheep suddenly surrounded me. It was strange, but I had never noticed their horns before; now one was piercing my leg and another at my ankles, they seemed much more fierce close up and much more powerful - I couldn't move - I was desperately trying to remain standing, 'shoo shoo' I squeaked, they moved a little then surrounded me with even more force. Clinging to the feedbag, I looked desperately towards my lecturer and classmates expecting to see them rushing down the hill to my aid, but they remained static whilst hundreds of sheep were attacking me. They seemed unaware of my terror. As I was about to scream for help, I heard what sounded like laughter, and I could just make out their faces – were they smiling? I turned back to the sheep and screamed 'GET OFF YOU PIGS!'

They scattered – I quickly filled the troughs then walked back to a rather smug group and tried not to show the relief on my face.

A few months after starting college, I was given the opportunity to move from my digs into a flat with two other girls from the class. I was excited about the prospect: Mr & Mrs D's constant concern about my well-being was becoming irritating and their children had proved to be less friendly than I'd first thought. They'd kindly invited me to spend Christmas with them which would save me travel money and although I would miss my family, I thought that spending Christmas in a different place would be fun. However, on Christmas morning I looked on in astonishment as their children showed little pleasure in receiving the most amazing gifts: instead they put a great deal of effort into counting them. They then complained to their parents about things they didn't receive before comparing gift values. Even though our Christmas meals were often blighted by my father staying in the pub while we sat waiting for him as the food went cold, I had never had such a miserable Christmas. Finally, the thought of not having to face Mrs D's porridge in the mornings was the decisive factor. Not long after moving in, she asked 'Do you like porridge?' Very foolishly I answered 'I love porridge' well, I did love porridge, the way my mother made it. At that point, I didn't realise there were different ways of making and eating porridge. Next morning there it was, waiting for me on the breakfast table, a huge mound, it was definitely a mound as it didn't move, just sat there in the centre of the plate not even attempting to touch the sides, a straight and solid mass of congealed oats. I was astonished as I pulled my seat towards it wondering how it would taste. Mr D sat opposite and cut out a similar mound for his plate, then to my utter amazement handed me a bowl of sugar, sugar! Where was the salt and for that matter the top of the milk? I shook my head to the sugar and forced a smile - somehow I got through the porridge and the rest of the day planning how to miss out on breakfast for the remainder of the winter.

I thought they'd be glad to get rid of me so didn't concern myself too much about telling them I was leaving - however, I hadn't considered the FREEZER. 'What will we do with all the food we have in the freezer?' hurtled Mrs D. 'Have you considered that?' I had never seen her so annoyed since the time I put an ink mark on my duvet cover. I had no reply. I knew nothing about freezers and certainly hadn't known she'd bought food for the year in advance. My mother bought our dinner daily; we never had more than one-day's food in the house, and that's if we were lucky. So no, I hadn't considered the freezer.

Then Wendy made matters worse by announcing she was also going to move digs to a place closer to the college. The atmosphere over the next week was not good. We sat with our heads bowed over the porridge as it stood mocking us, then crept to our room in early evening. Mr D remained pleasant but Mrs D never forgave us.

Later I realised it was the money they were going to miss that upset Mrs D. I would never have realised, because to me this family had everything, money could not have been a concern to them, but of course, as I later learned, money is a concern to everyone - few people ever have enough.

3

Creative produce

Sharing a flat with farmers' daughters had some extra benefits; they were all good cooks and frequently brought home-produce to the flat. However, my two flatmates had noted that they did all the cooking whilst I just enjoyed it then washed up afterwards. I thought this was a good arrangement but after some months, they suggested I should take my turn at the cooking. I didn't have much experience or need to cook until then, so I suggested I made the only thing I knew how; macaroni cheese. (As children there had been many weeks when we had almost lived on this or the cauliflower cheese version). They seemed happy with this suggestion; it would make a change from beef, duck and the other inspirational creations they produced.

I measured out the macaroni and boiled it until tender, my flatmates sat at the table in the corner of the living room enjoying the chance to let me do the cooking, I could hear them happily chatting away. I drained it, took the cheese from the fridge and grated it amongst the macaroni; I then mixed it with a wooden spoon, placed it in a large bowl and proudly took it through to the table. I had after all succeeded in not burning anything.

As I sat the bowl on the table, there was a strange silence as they stared at it, their eyes met and they turned to look at me: although this reaction did concern me a little, I dismissed it and then proudly started spooning the macaroni onto the plates and sat down to eat. We ate our dinner but with little conversation, and I felt a little disappointed that they hadn't thought to congratulate me on my efforts. Thereafter I thought no more of the subject and took little note of the fact that we went back to the previous cooking/cleaning arrangement. Some weeks later as I sat with a crowd of college friends discussing a rather unpopular member of class, one mentioned 'and have you seen how she cooks macaroni? There's no sauce! She just grates the cheese into the boiled macaroni!' The others gave astonished laughs, I couldn't laugh I just cringed and said nothing. Later, I asked ask a friend if she could give me cooking lessons. However, as if that hadn't been bad enough, I then proceeded to insult my mother the next time I went home when I told her that she had been cooking macaroni cheese wrong all of her life and that she should learn to make a cheese sauce. My mother was magnanimous in her reaction, saying very little, instead responding by cooking her usual wonderful macaroni cheese that evening with no sauce and then a few days later making perfect cheese sauce for another dish.

However, my lack of knowledge on the subject of food continued to catch me out on several more occasions. One of these happened after a couple of friends were discussing their favourite food and the word 'avocado' was mentioned. I had never heard of this but decided not to show my ignorance. Several days later as I stood in the queue at the green grocers, I noticed a whole tray of avocado pears. I wanted to educate myself and bought one for my dinner that evening. It took a bit of getting used to but I thought it tasted not too bad. When we were next discussing food – a very popular topic with farmers' daughters, I thought I could now add to the conversation. Nonchalantly I said, 'I love avocado; in fact I had one last night with raspberry ripple ice cream'. My friends' heads turned at once towards me, 'Ice cream!' They said in unison. Then Fiona added, 'It's supposed to be a starter, not a sweet!' Yet again, my attempt to impress on the subject of food failed miserably. Although I have since succeeded in producing a number of rather impressive meals, (in fact my ultimate success was first prize for a Raspberry Mousse at a Young Farmers' produce show - the sad thing about it was that I lived in the raspberry growing county of Perthshire and should have made it with fresh raspberries. However,

I didn't have any so I made it not only with tinned raspberries, but tinned raspberries that had been spilt on the kitchen table and then been scooped back into the moose). Cooking is still an area I prefer to avoid.

At college, money was a big problem, as it always had been. I couldn't get a grant; my mother never knew what my father earned but whatever it was, it prevented me from being awarded a grant. This was hard to understand, as most of the other students were from farming families, and in comparison to my family were obviously very well off. Yet, I was denied a grant whilst they were receiving up to £2000 per year. It seemed so unjust, and my mother obviously thought so too, even going to the length of making an appointment with our local MP, but all to no avail. I'd ask the other students how this could be? Their families had cars and they all seemed so well off, even going to private schools. Most didn't have an answer, though a couple of them said it was their accountant who did the paperwork and it was based on the farm profit, not their wage. 'No money' in accounting terms is very different from 'no money' in actual life.

My mother therefore sent me digs money every week from her wages and there was occasionally £2 left to spend on going out. This inevitably caused a lot of hardship at home for the rest of the family. So when the opportunity of a weekend job arose from a neighbour of Mr & Mrs D, I immediately jumped at it, thinking it could be the answer to all our problems. It was as a petrol pump attendant in a town about 20 miles away - Kirkcaldy. I agreed to start working the following weekend and every weekend thereafter. Both Saturday and Sundays, 9am till 10pm. Geoff, the owner appeared very pleasant; a tall, slim and good-looking man, he said little more than was necessary but took me to meet another employee who showed me the job.

I was to be paid 60p an hour, out of which I had to pay for my train fare and lunch. It didn't leave me very much but even a small amount made a difference. The work wasn't hard, just boring and tiring. I discovered Geoff was paying everyone else 75p an hour and felt rather hurt. I let it go as I thought he would probably increase my wage when I had shown how well I could do the job.

I'd naively believed that if I was honest with him about how much I needed the work, then he'd give me the job, but the reality was that when Geoff knew I needed the job, he also knew I wouldn't argue about my wage. There were no minimum wage limits and I'm sure I wasn't the only person in this position. Despite the fact he didn't increase my wage, I still worked very hard and honestly for him. The other staff told me of ways in which they cheated the till, I was shocked and would never have had the conscience to steal from him. They said he was stealing from them, they were just taking back what was theirs.

On one evening, it rained incessantly and I noticed a stand of batteries had been set outside on the forecourt. As I prepared to close up, I realised I would have to bring the batteries inside. I lugged them in, the rain felt like needles as it battered in, turning to hail from across the Firth of Forth. The petrol station stood at the edge of the Port Brae, making it open to some dramatic weather in the winter; on some occasions I experienced waves lashing over the barriers and slipping into the forecourt. I laid the batteries in a corner next to the shelves stacked with antifreeze and oil, then sat down to tally up my daily sheet of sweeties sold. Leaning my elbow on my knee, it slipped and a large whole appeared in my jeans - were they really that worn? I touched the hole and another appeared, and then another. My only pair of jeans began disintegrating in front of my eyes. Within minutes, I was no longer looking at Jeans, just red, bare legs. I was baffled, but then as I looked across the shop I noticed holes had appeared in the lino in a pattern that retraced my steps to where I had laid down the batteries. There had to be a connection and I concluded it must have been the rainwater from the batteries, which had somehow eaten holes in everything.

The rain had now turned to snow outside and I thought it would be easier to catch the bus home as there would be less people around than at the train station. I had a short duffle jacket with me and I wrapped it around my legs. I tried to run towards the bus because not only was I embarrassed, but I was very cold. I managed to avoid the stares of other passengers as I climbed aboard covered in snow from head to waist with my jacket wrapped around my legs.

When I arrived home, I learned from one of the other students that batteries contained acid. For the rest of the evening I worried what Geoff would say about his lino, but when I spoke to him the next day, he quickly changed the subject. I thought this was a sign of kindness and used the opportunity to suggest tentatively that he might give me something towards a new pair of jeans, but he ignored the remark. I therefore had to phone home and asked my mother if she could manage an extra £5 for jeans; she of course sent it with no mention of the problems it would cause at home that week and I only learned many years later that Geoff's silence on the matter came from his knowledge of employer legislation and that he should not have left me to move the batteries.

4

A Clyde sunset

Most students went home at weekends, therefore having the job kept me occupied when I would otherwise have been lonely on my own. However, I always looked forward to the longer holidays when I could go home and see my family.

During our Christmas holidays from college, I met my 'first love'. My sister was working in the hotel, which belonged to my Aunt and Uncle at Wemyss Bay and I went down to visit for a day before going back to college. Sis was going out with a guy from the village and he brought along a friend. We went out for a walk in the woods and I was completely in awe of him. He was tall, with dark hair that reached his shoulders and the most beautiful dark brown eyes. I was besotted, so when we returned to the hotel and he seemed genuinely sorry that I was going away to college, I was thrilled.

On returning to Cupar, I decided to write a letter and asked Wendy for help. It took over an hour to compose something, which wouldn't leave me looking too much of a fool if he chose to ignore it. The letter was fun, friendly, and I hoped he would reply.

I waited each day but nothing arrived in the post. I'd given up hope when after almost three weeks, there it was - a letter postmarked *Greenock*. I was elated, wrote back immediately and that was the start of a very romantic relationship. He later told me he'd tried for days to compose a response but without success. In the end he got very drunk and asked his sister to help him write the letter.

I discovered that one of the Farm Management students, Peter, who was rather hunky and fancied by most of the girls, lived near to my home. Of more importance to me was the fact that he had a car, a little mini clubman. Even more importantly, he went home most weekends. I built up the courage to approach Peter and ask if I could get a lift back to Bridge of Weir with him some weekends. He was very relaxed about it and agreed to take me with him the following weekend, so I arranged to have time off work. I sat in the car, very impressed with it. I knew nothing of cars, my family never owned one and I'd only ever been in a car when I was with my school friend and her parents. The car park was immediately behind the college and although never full, it was usually busy. Peter climbed in, ready to set off, but then spotted a friend; he climbed out to have a chat - suddenly the car began to move slowly downhill. I looked around at Peter and he shouted 'put on the handbrake!' My brain went into overdrive as I tried to guess what a handbrake looked like - I looked anxiously around me, the car was picking up speed; it was heading towards some other cars - I panicked and turned the steering wheel, then the horn blasted. The door swung open, Peter jumped in and pulled on the brake. We came to a halt about half an inch from another parked car. He looked at me in disbelief; he was red-faced and harassed but said nothing as we began our long journey home. I never asked him for another lift…and he never offered again.

I met my boyfriend at a local hotel along with my sister and two friends. It went well and he asked if we could keep writing to each other - I found it hard to believe this man actually wanted to go out with me. He was not only handsome and charming but he was obviously from a wealthy family – their house being one of the rare attractive ones, stone built in its own grounds; it even had a flagpole in the garden. It overlooked the Clyde and they owned part of the beach in front of the house, it didn't seem to make sense that he liked me. But he did, and the proof came on St Valentine's Day when I received my first ever valentine – it was huge, boxed, padded and had red roses on the front - just signed 'George'.

The exams came and went and then college finished

for the summer, I was glad to be home where I could see more of George. I managed to find a job at weekends cleaning in a local hotel. After work I would hitch a lift to Greenock; buses were very rare and although I hated hitching it was the only way to get about. George and I got on well over the holidays but the doubts I had about his reasons for liking me were never far from the surface; I would test his loyalty in silly ways by starting an argument just to see if he would say sorry, he always did, but the doubts remained.

My cleaning job at The Gryffe Hotel only lasted a couple of weeks, I was getting on fine but the housekeeper was having an affair with the manager, and he allowed her to treat the staff as she chose. There would be no pleasing her, the harder I worked, the more she found something to complain about. She had taken an early dislike to me and I was certain she intentionally gave me the worst jobs. One of these was to clean the male toilets, not only the ones in the upstairs hall but also in downstairs bar, which were always in a mess. Then one day as I was about to finish, she told me to go back and clean the windowsills, as I'd missed some dust. I refused and argued with her, so she went to the manager to complain, and I followed on: he said nothing, just shrugged his shoulders as we both gave our sides of the argument. His nonchalant response made my blood boil and I blew up; lambasting him for the way the jobs were allocated and his unfairness. He looked at me stunned and then, slightly bemused as I walked out saying I wouldn't be back. I now had to sign on to the 'brew', something I hoped never to do. It was a bus journey to Linwood; a lifeless concrete block. As I sat in the grey offices waiting my turn behind a queue of forlorn looking young women with greetin kids and hopeless looks, I promised myself it would be the last time and I would ever be like that.

The summer holidays came to a close and George and I talked about our future. One evening we sat on the beach watching the sun set over the Clyde, it was a beautiful sunset, very red, so red it made a roadway on the water. 'Will you marry me?' said George. He stared straight ahead, watching the sunset, never turning to me. I wasn't sure if I had heard him correctly, I looked at him until he turned his head and looked at me: then I began to laugh; there was no way he could seriously want to marry me after all.

George tried to persuade me not to go back to college, if I stayed, his parents would buy us a flat in Greenock. However, I would never consider leaving college, I desperately wanted a career, I needed to feel I could support myself. My mother had been trapped in a marriage because she was unable to cope on her own financially, I couldn't let that happen to me.

A week later, a few days before I went back to college, George and I split up. Nothing final was ever said we just stopped contacting each other.

5

Fuel for thought

By the time I returned to college, my mother had separated from my father and I was able to get the full student grant. Mum used some of it to pay off rent arrears run up by my father, but now at least I could afford a little bit more than the year before.

I was looking forward to being able to enjoy my weekends. Unexpectedly however, a few days after returning to college, Geoff rang and asked if I would work for him once again at the petrol station. Although not keen, I agreed as I didn't want to let him down. I soon realised my loyalty was one sided as I discovered my wages were still to be 60p an hour.

A month later it was my 18th birthday and I was working in the garage, feeling a little fed up and missing my family. It was nearly 10pm, closing time, when the telephone rang; it was Geoff. He asked if I would keep the station open an extra half hour and he would pick me up. I agreed reluctantly but said I would go for the last train as I knew from experience he would be late and it would probably be after 11pm before he arrived.

I worked on until 10.30pm. Then, just as I was turning off the lights, a car drew in. The man got out and pleaded with me to serve him some petrol as he was completely empty - I didn't have the heart to say no. This was before self-service, so I trundled back out into the dark and quickly filled his tank and then another car drew in. I told him I was closed but he too pleaded and reluctantly I also served him.

Now, racing about to lock the door, I began worrying about the time: if I was to catch the last train I was going to have to run. It must have been about a mile to the station and I ran most of the way, but as I rushed through the entrance I saw the train leave. Now what? Still out of puff, I decided to run back to the petrol station in case Geoff called in on his way home. When I got back, there was no sign he had been, so I waited and waited but he never arrived. I telephoned his house but there was no answer. By midnight I realised I would have to spend the night in the station. I was starving and tired, I found an old blanket in the storeroom but there was nowhere comfortable to lie, I sat down on the concrete floor and cried. In despair, I committed a crime – I took a packet of fruit pastilles, which I didn't pay for and ate them slowly throughout the night. I telephoned my mother from the telephone call box, which was on the wall of the station shop. She felt helpless as I sobbed down the phone, what a way to spend my 18th birthday.

A few weeks later Geoff asked if I would work until 11pm on Sundays. 'No' I said, 'there are no trains at that time'. He tried to assure me he would always pick me up but I still refused: thirteen hours without a break was long enough. Twenty minutes later the telephone rang, it was Geoff's wife. I had never met or spoken to her before, so was surprised when she said who she was. She said it was important that the station remained open until 11pm. However, although she came over very sweet and persuasive, I wouldn't budge, there was no way I was prepared to work that late. Then her tone changed, 'you don't have a say in it', she insisted, 'we are keeping the station open until 11pm on Sundays and you'll just have to work until then'.

I put down the receiver, astonished by her remarks. I became angry. I couldn't believe someone I'd never met could talk to me in such a manner. After a few minutes I rang her back and told her I wanted to leave and wouldn't be in the following weekend. She was furious, 'you can't leave at such short notice', but the ruder she became, the more determined I was to go. 'Well, I've no choice, something has come up and I can't work next weekend'. I could hardly believe my own reaction, I always tried to please people, accepting less than reasonable treatment without complaint and suddenly I was standing up to someone, and not giving in. I found myself responding with clarity at every comment she made. There was a final silence and I put the telephone down. Then surprisingly, Geoff arrived before closing time to give me a lift home - this was a first. Once again he asked me not to leave, but still there was to be no compromise on the hours, I had to work until 11pm. I suggested I could do Saturdays only, but he wouldn't discuss any other option. I knew I could manage on my grant and had only gone back to work to help him, but he wasn't aware of my new situation. I was to take it or leave it - so I left it. He drove me home in his small, white sports car. I liked cars and being driven fast but Geoff drove at such a speed I couldn't move my head, it was firmly pinned back against the seat. He drove through the darkness of the country roads in silence and I cringed as I saw the speedometer pass 100 mph. I was terrified, which I'm sure was his intention. At every corner I closed my eyes and my fingers clung tightly to the smooth white leather of the seat; the headlights flashed through the trees that lined the roadside and I was acutely aware of stone walls lining the roads. I began to think that perhaps I should work an extra hour after all. To my great relief we finally arrived home safely; as I climbed out of the car I said 'thank you', then 'goodbye', but he never responded. I didn't hear from him again, but a few weeks later Mrs D told me he'd been badly injured on the same road when he hit the back of a broken-down tractor.

6

Strangers in the night

My train from Glasgow to Edinburgh was late, I ran across the platform dragging a very large case and some extra bags, but I was too late, I had missed my connection for Cupar. At the ticket desk I was told there would be no more trains tonight. There was, however, a train to Leuchars which was about 10 miles from Cupar, so I decided I could get that one and hire a taxi into Cupar.

I arrived in Leuchars about 11pm; it was dark and drizzly and I was the only person to disembark onto the tiny platform. I asked the Stationmaster where I could find a telephone and he pointed in the direction of the village. So with case and bags I headed down a cobbled path towards the small and dark village. I found the 'phone box and took out my purse but I only had a single 2p coin. However, I thought that would be enough to make one call. I rang a firm which had its number on the inside of the 'phone box; they were from nearby St Andrews so I didn't think I would have long to wait. However, when they answered they told me I would have to wait half an hour as they were busy. As I didn't have other options, I agreed to wait and went outside. The only light was from the 'phonebox, the sky was black, no moon or stars to be seen; a breeze got up and I pulled my duffle coat tighter around me as I sat on my case and waited, and waited and waited. It was now 12.30am and I realised the taxi firm must have forgotten about me. I walked back to the station to get more change but it was in darkness. Then it started to rain, a fine smir, enough to dampen the air. What could I do? It seemed I had no choice but to walk along to the main Cupar Road and try to hitch a lift. I walked about a mile with my case and bags before I reached the main road; my arms were aching and my clothes were beginning to feel damp and I was worried about hitching. I walked about a mile before I saw any sign of a vehicle; as it came closer I put out my hand but it drove past. My years of hitchhiking experience had taught me that only a few people are prepared to pick up a stranger. I lifted my case and continued, the rain was getting heavier and Cupar was at least another six miles away. Another vehicle came and once again I put out my hand to thumb the lift, but it too passed. Then after some distance I saw its brake lights go on and it stopped and began reversing back to me; this filled me with both relief and terror. A middle-aged man opened the passenger door and leaned over the seat, 'Where are you going?' he queried with some puzzlement across his face. I responded 'Cupar'. He said he wasn't going that far but would take me as far as he could. He then climbed out and placed my bags in his boot. 'I only changed my mind and stopped when I realised you were a woman'. He explained. I thanked him and tried to smile. I then sat in the passenger seat hugging the door close and planning my imminent escape. I didn't want to say much but he seemed friendly so I explained what had happened. As we arrived close to his destination, he said. 'I may as well take you into Cupar but I'll need to let my wife know' and at that he turned the car into a small, dark caravan park. As he drove between the narrow, empty lanes of the park, I felt terror rising, I desperately tried to envisage what I would do if anything awful happened. I was trying to decide at what point to open the car door and run when he came to a stop and jumped out. He then entered a small caravan that showed no signs of life, but to my great relief, a small light was switched on before he jumped back into the driver's seat and said, 'well, that's sorted'. It wasn't long before we arrived in Cupar. Still not fully trusting him, I asked to be dropped off about half a mile from my house. Once out on the pavement, and on retrieving my bags, I offered him a pound note for his petrol but he kindly refused. 'Thank you, goodnight'. I said, and headed towards my flat as he turned and drove off.

It was such a relief to be back in Cupar, only a short walk, then out of the rain and into a warm bed. It was now 2 am. I climbed the steps to my flat, dropped my case and bags on the doorstep and looked into my purse, then my handbag, and then through every pocket. Eventually I emptied out my case and bags onto the damp steps until I finally came to the conclusion I had forgotten my keys.

Completely exhausted, both physically and mentally, I sat on the doorstep feeling numb. At least I had some shelter as there was a small canopy across the steps between my door and the neighbours, but it was February, and it was cold. I put on another jumper and huddled against the wall until I dozed off. The sound of footsteps running up the stairs woke me with a jolt; I looked up in surprise to see an even more surprised milkman looking down at me. 'What happened to you?' he quizzed. After a short explanation, he went off and reappeared with two plain rolls and a pint of milk. He handed them to me and said 'you look like you might be glad of these', and I certainly was. It was now 5 am; my flatmates would be travelling from home straight to college, so I would have to wait until college began before I could get a key and finally get inside.

To pass the time, I took a walk through Cupar; it was strange being around when everyone else was in bed, it seemed different at this time of day. I came across a chocolate machine and needed to find some change:

then I spotted a lady looking as though she was going or coming back from a cleaning job; a scarf tied round her hair and an apron on. I approached her and asked for change, and she managed to find some, seeming unconcerned about meeting me. What a wonderful taste that bar of chocolate had.

Eventually, when I arrived at College and recounted my experience of the night before, everyone seemed to have an idea of what I should have done; from going to the police, to waking our neighbours (who had a spare key). Somehow, none of them seemed so realistic at 2am.

7

Finding my feet

I was unaware that the career I had chosen in agriculture was another area where I'd encounter both class divide and chauvinism. At school I had had two friends from farms, however, in the West of Scotland farming is quite poor and the place is not a great agricultural area, we tended to look with sympathy on our farming friends who appeared even poorer than ourselves. This was not the case in the East of Scotland. Here, farming was one of the main industries, the farms were large and often wealthy, and it was they who looked down on the 'townies'.

I had made friends easily at college and although I did feel a little out of place at times amongst a class of farmers' daughters, it didn't cause me any problems. The majority were friendly, but my naivety saved me on more than one occasion from the jokes of the men: I couldn't understand their attitude towards me, often being derisory and mocking. They didn't understand why I, 'a townie', was on such a course. I think they thought the women on the course should only be there to find a suitable husband, and as farming men, they were only going to marry suitable farming women, so there was little point in my being there. Most of them would never have considered the idea that a woman might be on the course to learn something, and then make use of that knowledge in a career. It is true that some of the women on the course were just passing time until they found someone to marry - and that someone would ideally be a farmer of means. A few of the ladies were open about this and told me it was the reason that their parents had agreed to them attending college.

One night early in the course, a group of us sat in the local pub chatting, Hamish sat opposite, he was a small chap, had small eyes and a large jaw, thickly built, he was liked by many of the girls, which I couldn't understand and to my dismay was the boyfriend of my closest friend, Wendy. I think he sensed my puzzlement. He definitely had no time for me. He pulled out a piece of paper from his pocket and handed it to one of the girls, she laughed loudly then passed it on, as it went around the group, each would laugh in turn, then finally it was handed to me; it was a joke. I began to read it when Hamish snatched it from my hand. 'You won't understand it', he snapped. I didn't respond because he was quite right, although I had seen much more in my life than most of them ever would, they knew much more about sex than I did. However, on this occasion, as on many others, I felt they believed that lack of knowledge also meant a lack of brains.

I had such a different approach to life, and found it odd to discover people could judge you by your wellies, but this they did. I wore three quarter black ones and this was a great source of humour for many of my classmates who wore green wellies with little buckles on the side. The buckles served no particular purpose, or at least none that I have ever discovered. Why was the colour of their wellies important when none of them bothered to put make-up on? Were farming men more impressed by their partner's feet than their faces? It seemed to be so. However, feeling the need to fit in, I abandoned the make-up but my black wellies had to remain.

Mostly the girls enjoyed telling me about their lifestyles and would occasionally ask me to visit their homes. One such visit took me to a farm near Jedburgh. The farmhouse was wonderful, just as I imagined a farmhouse to look, the large hot Aga in the kitchen, lots of wellies at the door, (notably not all green) large cosy chairs everywhere and the smell of home cooking lingering throughout the house.

Even my friend's mother looked as I imagined a farmer's wife to be, fairly small and chubby with cheery, red cheeks and she usually wore a large, floral cotton apron.

The first morning we arrived in the kitchen to cups of tea, lots of toast and a cooked breakfast of sausages and bacon. We sat at a wooden table that dominated the kitchen and I thought how wonderful it must be to live here – then there was a knock at the door - Jane said 'Oh that will be our postman, Bert'. (imagine knowing his name, I thought). Jane went towards the door and I followed behind. As she opened the door she was greeted by a very friendly looking postman with a large smile. 'Oh hello there, how are you getting on at college then?' He asked. Jane replied, and then turned towards me, this is a friend from college, Hazel. He turned to me smiling and stepped forward ready to greet me, 'she's from Glasgow' said Jane as I said 'Hello' in my Glasgow accent. At that, his smile disappeared and he stepped slightly back. He eyed me suspiciously. I was stunned by his reaction for the rest of the day - did he think I was going to take a knuckle duster out and mug him because I was from Glasgow? Did my accent really give such a bad impression?

That look and reaction from the postman was not uncommon, I must have looked reasonably friendly because at first sight people would react positively, however, as soon as I spoke their reactions would change. Years later when I was married and looking to buy my first house, I saw a bungalow with a 'for sale' sign outside, so I rang the number, explained my interest in the house and asked how much they were looking for? There was a loud laugh and the man on the other end of the line said, 'well, it won't be anything you can afford', then he put the phone down on me. Initially, I tried to change my accent, but over time such reactions made me highlight it more.

Whilst I was in Jedburgh, Jane took me on a visit to an aunt's farm. The elderly lady lived alone on an isolated hill farm; she worked it by herself after her husband had died many years previously and despite the protests from her family. I was in complete awe of this lady, she had the largest and roughest hands I had seen on any person, let alone a woman, yet she was very gentle and feminine. Even though she was old, she appeared to be more alive than anyone I had ever met. The lines on her face, thick grey tangled hair and yet a softness in her voice and eyes made her special. It was as though she had been brought to life from a story book.

Her life was hard, the farm being high on the Border hills – a beautiful place in the summer but a harsh life in winter. The house was dimly lit and although filled with furniture it was not luxury, stone floors and rattling windows. She spoke about the lambing and her worry of the weather becoming colder. She complained about the rabbits, so much damage to the young grass, she had shot a few the evening before but she expected it would make little difference. I could see why so many country people found it hard to relate to those from the towns; their entire existence being so different. My own beliefs of country life were being rapidly dismantled and rebuilt, sometimes rather uncomfortably.

I began to realise many country people thought the only way of protecting themselves was to put up barriers, yet to me it was the taking down of these barriers that opened my eyes. This acquiring of knowledge was a two-way thing, I was learning about the countryside way of life and my friends were discovering that not everyone from the town with a Glasgow accent was a hooligan.

8

Standing on my own

Everyone hated our English Communication class: the lecturer was the cause of this, all students disliked him, he shouted, was rude and gave excessive work. It was only one lesson a week but even then, it was too much for most of us.

On this afternoon, we were listening to him talk about the various ways the same stories were reported in different newspapers. I found this interesting: he had several papers and we read the same news story from each, and then he highlighted how each paper had emphasised different aspects of the story. I sat at the back of the class; four rows were in front of me. He was a large slightly rotund man, with not much hair. He never seemed to smile and his voice was droll. He then lifted a copy of The Daily Record, which was the paper my mother read. He said 'this is the kind of paper the working classes read, as you will notice the news is printed in words of no more than two syllables

- this is all they are able to read or understand'.

With that remark he carried on to another paper but I wasn't listening any more. I was very angry; I could feel the blood rising to my cheeks. He had insulted my mother. My mother who was an expert at crosswords and probably knew more words in the English dictionary than everyone in the room put together. My mother who read Chaucer, Burns *and* The Daily Record.

He then strolled to his desk and sat down as he told us to begin our essay on the subject. The class unaware of my outrage began to write. So did I, but I was not at all happy, and couldn't let such a remark go unchallenged. I laid my pen on the desk and sat up straight. Wendy beside me, nudged me with her elbow and whispered 'what are you doing?' I just shook my head. Everyone was busy writing and then he looked up from his desk and noticed me sitting staring at the ceiling. At first he looked puzzled but did not say anything, his eyes looked back down to his desk and he continued to write. I sat up straighter, and this time he looked up and took notice. 'What are you doing there, girl? You cannot be finished your essay already'. I could feel my hands beginning to shake; his voice was powerful. 'I am finished Sir, because I do not know enough two syllable words to write anything further'. At that, a sea of heads lowered towards their desks, I felt even more vulnerable now, but I had gone this far. He was taken aback by my remark and unsure of what to do. 'Don't be silly, girl, get on with your work', he hesitated, and then looked down to his desk. 'Not until you apologise'. I heard myself saying with some surprise. There was a deafening silence and an atmosphere of unease. 'Bring your jotter out here now!' he tried to appear angry, but I suspect he was more amazed than annoyed. I rose and took my few lines to his desk; several people were courageous enough to look up as he looked at my work and pointed to a sentence. 'See, these all have more than two syllables in them, you can write more'. I nodded. 'Yes', I said, 'exactly, we working class people do have a better vocabulary than you said'.

'It was not meant to be a serious remark', he snapped, before handing back the book. 'Now go and sit down and finish your work. 'I had made my point, so I sat down and finished my essay. If he had made the remark to try and provoke a response, I think he got more than he bargained for. The next day going to college, I was greeted by many students, 'well done' they said, 'we heard what you did'. I was amazed, everyone in college seemed to have heard about the episode, but as in Chinese whispers, the story circulating had now changed; it seemed that most people thought I had retorted that I couldn't think of enough four letter words to write. After things settled down, the lecturer and I got on well. A few weeks later, I heard his daughter was unwell with leukaemia, I felt sad for him, perhaps he had good reason to be an angry person.

9

A Toe in the line

I stood at the end of the queue, it was a lovely day, the sky was blue but it was not too warm. I had been feeling a little nervous so I bought a packet of glacier mints on my way to the bus stop. This was my first interview, I had applied for the job from the local paper, not because I wanted the job but I thought I stood a good chance of obtaining an interview and we'd been told to get lots of interview practice. The job was for a clerical assistant in an accountant's office, not what I was looking for, I wanted to become a farm secretary on a large farming unit. I didn't like the idea of travelling around the countryside to different farms, so decided that I would take a job at one place only.

I was early, so had time to buy some sweets for the journey. I stood in the bus queue grateful for a dry, sunny day and popped a glacier mint into my mouth. It immediately slipped down my throat. I tried to cough it up, but it lodged further down - I turned to the lady next to me, but she turned away as the bus rumbled to a stop. I could breathe but with difficulty. A yellow van crept along the busy road and I jumped off the pavement and caught hold of the open window pointing to my throat. Tears poured down my cheeks. 'Get in - I'll take you to the Health Centre', said the elderly male driver. I gladly obeyed.

On arrival at the Health Centre, I had difficulty explaining the problem. The nurse called the doctor and said. 'She has a Polo mint stuck in her throat'. I shook my head but couldn't explain it wasn't a Polo Mint but a larger mint. The doctor seemed amused, and asked me to lie on the examination table in order to peer down my throat with a small torch. To my amazement he summoned an ambulance to take me to the nearest hospital - twenty miles in the opposite direction of my interview. This added to my upset and I handed the nurse my interview letter. After reading it, she said. 'Don't worry, I'll telephone to explain you'll be late'.

The ambulance driver suggested I sat in the front of the ambulance, which I did so willingly. I stared ahead clinging to my throat as we sped along the country roads of Fife. He began to chuckle to himself. 'A Polo mint, imagine a Polo mint sticking in your throat. If that's what a Polo mint does, it's just as well for you it wasn't one of those Foxes Glacier mints'. I didn't try to correct this.

On arrival at the hospital, I was clearly not an emergency. I sat feeling out of place in my business suit amongst the cut and bruised of Kirkcaldy. An hour passed, then to my horror I realised the mint had melted. I sneaked towards the reception to tell them my problem had resolved itself, but before I could explain, I heard my name called. The entire waiting room watched with curiosity as I entered a small cubicle where a doctor awaited.

I explained to the young, male doctor what had happened emphasising the pain I had been in but that the mint had now melted. He stared at me in silence. I assured him I would manage to recover adequately. He was impassive. I fell silent too. He then walked out of the cubicle. The nurse looked at me with a mix of bemusement and pity. I waited to be told I could leave, but the doctor reappeared carrying a glass of water, handed it to me, turned and left. Somehow, I didn't feel he sympathised with my plight. I eventually returned home in an ambulance, which collected elderly patients from various areas around Kirkcaldy. Most of the journey consisted of me explaining to each new passenger why I was there and the horrors of glacier mints. Each explanation was met with amazement, and the assurance that they had sucked glacier mints on a regular basis for years with no such mishaps.

Two hours after the original interview time I called the accountant, who seemed unperturbed and said I should come along anyway. Friends told me that Blairgowrie was a small village situated just after Alyth. So after passing Alyth I disembarked at the next village and popped into a nearby shop to ask for directions. 'Oh, that must be in Blairgowrie', said the lady. Seeing my jaw drop, she added 'it's only a couple of miles', as if to reassure me.

My new, high-heeled shoes were not worn in, and became very noticeable during the walk. The sun was warm and the knitted, woollen suit that was supposed to make me look smart was now causing me to overheat. My throat hurt, and I was late again.

As I arrived in the main square (I later discovered this was called the Wellmeadow), I spotted a group of young people sitting on a wall chatting. I approached them to ask for directions and was amazed to hear them respond in broad Glaswegian accents. It turned out that Blairgowrie was a popular place for Glasgwegians to visit in the summer to work on the many berry farms in the area. I eventually found the office on the first floor above a ski shop. It smelled of new paint and bleach. The accountant appeared friendly and unconcerned by my secondary lateness. He showed me to an interview room, offered a chair at a neat, modern desk and sat opposite. The desk contained a notepad and small cube games. I wondered if they were to be part of the interview – I didn't think I stood any hope of getting the balls in the hoops.

The events of the day had wiped out my motivation and now, without nerves, I heard myself respond to questions in a confident and sometimes cheeky manner. With each answer, I wanted to look over my shoulder to see who had spoken. 'Would you ever consider training as an accountant?' He asked. 'No, if I'd wanted to be an accountant I would have trained as one'. I replied. He seemed shocked by my answers - they astounded me. However, the job sounded interesting and I began to wish I had taken it seriously.

When finished, he thanked me and shook my hand. I moved towards the top of the stairs and turned to say goodbye. 'Don't go eating any more mints'. he said smiling. I laughed, turned, and fell down the stairs.

The letter arrived the next week offering me the job. I wondered how my unusual entrance and departure had affected his decision. I concluded he had to be either very brave, or completely crazy. As it transpired, he required both of these skills.

10

Lodgers and lawyers

One of the farm management students hailed from Blairgowrie and offered me the use of a caravan on his father's farm. When college finished, I packed up all my belongings including my cat into a special box and my friend Rhona gave me a lift to Blairgowrie. We passed the famous Beech Hedge at Meikleour, the tallest hedge in the world, so tall that I didn't realise I was looking at it. When we arrived at the farm, I had to knock for several minutes before my college friend very sheepishly opened the door. He looked at me awkwardly and then said 'sorry, but my Dad says we need to keep the caravan for the berry pickers'. I never saw any glimpse of his father as he closed the door and left me standing. There was nothing for it but to go into Blairgowrie and find a Bed & Breakfast. Rhona dropped me off in the centre of the town at the tourist information office. She then had to head off on her long drive to the Black Isle. She wished me luck. The tourist office was in the Wellmeadow; the central area of Blairgowrie. I explained my plight to two elderly ladies behind the counter and asked if they had details of any cheap bed and breakfast accommodation. After a bit of chat, they suggested I contact a lady who worked with them, as she was considering taking in a lodger. They rang her for me and let me speak to her. She agreed to meet me at her house which was on the outskirts of the town, in a modern development. I set off with bags and my cat in its box. On arriving at the house, an elderly woman holding a zimmer frame greeted me. She explained she suffered from MS and invited me in to see what would be my bedroom; a small but pleasant room that smelt of moth balls. I was so glad to have somewhere to stay that I didn't question anything as she listed what I could and could not do and the rent of £4 per week seemed reasonable. Once again, I was lodging in a shiny but rather grey Scottish house.

After a few months, I started looking for my own place. Miss Mac was a nice enough lady but she was another person who wanted to fuss over me. She would always ask where I was going and who I was with. She insisted that I ate my meals with her and always decided what we would eat. If I was out in the evenings, she would wait up until I came in, which made me feel obliged not to be too late. Over the next few weeks, it became clear that Miss Mac was looking for a companion rather than a lodger. She tried to involve me in her life by introducing me to the Women's Institute. On one occasion, she invited several members to the house and asked me to make scones for the tea party. My heart sank at this request and I wondered if I should warn her about my cooking disasters, but then she should have warned me that her bag of flour was so old that it was probably pre-war. When I handed out the scones, the look on the faces of her visitors told me that there was a high possibility that I might be shot if I ever considered joining the WI. After the guests left, we agreed that cardboard would probably have tasted better. I did feel sorry for Miss Mac, as a spinster with MS, she didn't have much to be cheery about but then it wasn't my responsibility to try and change that. In the end I had to escape her gloom. The final straw came when we heard an owl one night and she told me that it was a sign of death and someone would die soon. Ten minutes later my mother 'phoned to say my sister had had a severe asthma attack and had nearly died. When I told the news to Miss Mac, I thought she looked rather too smug.

A few weeks later, I saw a flat advertised in the local paper. I managed to get the rent of it with the help of my boss who suggested I offer £18 per week instead of the £15 being asked. I took his advice and made an appointment with the solicitor. When I met Mr McPherson for the first time, I immediately felt intimidated by his large frame, dark suit and rather severe expression. His office was gloomy and the walls were panelled with a stained wood. He sat behind a large desk, which was completely covered in files and papers. Heaps of these files sat around the room, stacked precariously high and leaning in on each other. The room itself was large but there was very little space to be seen anywhere. He seemed a huge man but I think this was more in his demeanour than his physique. He was so serious he terrified me into almost complete silence. After I'd offered the extra rent and answered questions on my work, he agreed to let me have the flat. I stood up ready to leave, yet he continued writing and then without looking at me, said, 'there's not many people who could last more than a week in the company of Miss Mac'. I didn't know how to respond, he continued writing and I just nodded my acknowledgment and then turned and left. I wasn't looking forward to telling Miss Mac that I was leaving, but I now felt a bit better about it. I was delighted to have my own place at last. The flat was above another of the town's ski shops and had a garden to the back, which my cat, spud, would enjoy and there were elderly neighbours on both sides. All I had to do was find a flatmate and a college friend who'd moved to the area to be near her boyfriend had already said she was interested.

Finally, everything seemed to be working out well, a good job, a nice flat in a lovely area, and I was already making new friends through the Young Farmers' club. I was very happy. Most of all I would soon be able to help the rest of my family financially, and had already done so by paying my Mum's flight to Scotland to see my sister in hospital.

11

A foot in the mouth

I'd been settled in the flat a couple of months when one evening as I made tea the phone rang and I went through to the living room to answer it. It was my mum and after we talked, I sat down to watch TV. A short time later, I smelt burning and opened the door to see the hall full of thick smoke. I ran through to the kitchen and saw flames leaping out of the chip pan. I grabbed a towel, soaked it in water and flung it over the pan before opening the door and windows.

The black smoke was everywhere; the cooker had melted, as had the window blinds and the wall clock. I telephoned friends and they came down to help. There wasn't much we could do to clean the black, sticky mess, which had infiltrated every nook and cranny. The next day I had to tell Mr McPherson what had happened. I was literally shaking in my shoes when I entered his office. As I sat in front of his overbearing and laden desk again, I quietly explained that I had accidentally ruined much of the lovely flat he had recently let to me. I was surprised when he didn't rage as his demeanour would have suggested, instead he asked about my house insurance and explained that I should make a claim immediately and to make sure I put all the details in and not miss anything out. He scribbled a list as we talked, making suggestions about items that should be checked and claimed. He seemed quite matter of fact about it all and it was a great relief to me. My insurance covered most of the repairs, the kitchen and hall were redecorated and the flat looked better than when we moved in.

About a month later, whilst preparing tea one evening, I answered the telephone to my boyfriend, we fell out and I put the phone down running upstairs to my bedroom. Lying on my bed feeling sorry for myself, I heard shouting from below and went to investigate. I couldn't believe my eyes - there was smoke everywhere again - the chips! I had forgotten about them again and this time, luckily, my neighbours had spotted the smoke. This fire seemed worse and although I tried to throw a wet towel across it, the smoke was too thick so I telephoned the fire brigade.

As the brigade clanged its way to my flat, my boss, Graham, happened to be driving along behind it. He turned to his girlfriend and joked, 'that'll be on its way to another of Hazel's chip pan fires'. When he heard the next day that it had been, he was speechless.

Worse than the fire was the fact I had to face the terrifying Mr McPherson once again and tell him I had caused yet another fire. I was convinced he would evict me immediately, but not before reaching over the desk and tearing me apart, limb by limb. It took me all day to work up the courage to go and see him. I sat in the dark, cluttered room, staring through the tunnel of files at his stern expression, like a giant from a book of fairytales, he sat ready to pounce. He looked over his spectacles and began to get impatient for me to speak. 'I'm afraid I've had another chip pan fire', I squirmed, as all my prepared excuses vanished. Then there was the loudest roar of laughter I have ever heard. I'm sure my heart stopped. It took a few seconds before I could believe he was actually laughing. Mr McPherson then lifted a notepad, and now chuckling and shaking his head, he asked for details about how it happened. He then said he would make the claim on the Landlord's house insurance this time and instructed me to hand in all the repair receipts. Still chuckling, he waved me away. The relief I felt as I left the office was unbelievable and the look on the faces of his two receptionists was a picture.

I soon felt settled in Blairgowrie with my new job. It wasn't a farm secretary's job but because Blairgowrie was so rural, there were many farming clients, so I was able to use the agricultural training I had, to some extent. In fact, my boss found my agricultural knowledge very useful. I came armed with the Scottish Agricultural Handbook and the standard issue manual of agricultural chemicals. This book contained a list of all the Herbicide, Insecticide and Fungicides approved for use on farms with notes on their dilution and use, as well as their various commercial names. In 1979 this still included DDT as well as many other chemicals which were soon to be banned. Lectures at college had emphasised the importance of these chemicals in increasing profits and although they highlighted detrimental effects if people were over-exposed to them, there was no mention ever made of the growing concern about the effect they were having on the wildlife, let alone the long-term effects on humans. I was also working on the cusp of a major change in financial support to farmers. Yields had been increasing across all produce and farmer's were guaranteed a sale by the European Union, even if there was no market. This lead to huge over-production and the famous butter and grain mountains.

Although many young farmers were keen to modernise their family farms by going to college and learning new management and business methods, many of the old-time farmers continued farming in the way they'd been shown by their forefathers. One such farmer came to our office for help. He was nearing retirement age and by sheer chance, whilst investigating a haulage company, the Inland Revenue discovered his existence. He had never completed any paperwork for anything in all his years as a pig farmer. Instead, he'd bought and sold entirely by cash. But the times had caught up with him and now, Her Majesty's

Revenue wanted their dues. In the end, he could not alter his ways, and despite our best efforts to help, no paperwork was ever forthcoming. His farm was finally impounded by the Revenue and he lost everything. I was surprised by the powers of the Revenue to enter a house and remove anything they deemed important, not only in this case but on others that followed. Many things in Agriculture were changing, and in a small way, I was to be part of these changes: This was also the year Margaret Thatcher was voted in as Prime Minister, to my later lifelong regret, my first vote went to her in the belief that a strong woman would do wonderful things for women as a whole.

12

Foot on the pedal

Not long after settling in Blairgowrie, I decided it was time to continue my driving lessons. I started them at college but they came to an abrupt end when the instructor put his hand on my knee and offered me free lessons in the evenings. Everyone seemed to drive, and my boss thought I should have a driving licence as I would be able to visit clients without him. I tried three different instructors with varying degrees of upset, but as there were only three, I eventually had to go back to the first one. He was rather nervy and shouted a lot; on one occasion I arrived back at the office in tears - I had been driving towards a junction when he said, 'break, break, BREAK!' But he made me so nervous, I pressed the accelerator instead (there were no dual controls).There was a lorry heading towards us, so I moved my foot to the break but before I had the chance to press it, he thumped his foot down on top of mine bringing us to a sudden halt. I limped into the office, 'I am not going out with that mad man again'. I said.

I returned to the second instructor and we seemed to get on better this time. Quite quickly he suggested I should book my test. Despite being advised by several people to wait, I went ahead and booked a date. On reflection, I think the instructor was just desperate to get rid of me. A week before the test, a friend from the young farmers offered to give me a lesson in her car. I gladly accepted and we went out one evening when it was fairly quiet. As we approached a 'Give Way' and I indicated to turn right, she suddenly hauled on the handbrake and brought us to a stop, 'what's wrong?' I puzzled. She looked shaken 'I didn't think you were going to get round the corner' she said, looking at the wall ahead of us. I drove back slowly and the lesson came to an end. 'Perhaps you should put your test off a bit' she advised.

However, I remained hopeful and the test day arrived. I was nervous but the test itself went well with only one emergency stop when a bus pulled out in front of me. However, I started the engine up again and drove on. At the end, when the examiner said I'd passed, I was too scared to say anything. I just took the paper and walked away as fast as I could in case he changed his mind. Having taken time off work, I immediately went back to the office desperate to tell someone I had passed. I walked into the office and sat down. Graham never looked up, he continued with what he was doing then started discussing work, 'aren't you going to ask how I got on at my test?' I said, feeling deflated. 'Why, how did you get on, he quizzed?' 'I passed!' The look of utter amazement on his face said it all.

That evening when I rang around my friends, their reactions were all similar, no one mentioned the test until I did, then when I said I had passed, I could hear the silent shock. By the end of the night I thought I should go back to the examiner and ask if he was sure he hadn't made a mistake.

Now I had a driving licence, I wanted to buy a car. The prospect of the freedom a car would give me was thrilling and it was apparent no-one else would lend me theirs. I visited my bank manager. He was great, not only lending me money for a car, but he contacted a local garage and told them to look out for a suitable small vehicle for a young woman who had £500 to spend. A mini was found and delivered to their local garage for my inspection; the garage was just across the road from my new flat, so after work I went to see it. I walked around the bronze coloured mini; it seemed to have everything: four wheels, seats and windows, so I wrote the cheque. Mr Peterkin, my friendly Bank Manager had managed to get £75 off the price. I was so pleased and thought how great it was to have a bank manager, and wondered why everyone didn't have one.

My next problem was to drive the car across the road and park it outside my flat. By the time I sat in the driving seat, four mechanics had gathered to look on. I started it up and moved off; it stalled. I started it again and it hopped forward a few yards before it stalled again. I was aware of the eyes and smiles on me. Once again, I started the car and eventually after several starts and hops I crossed the road and brought the car to a stop outside my flat. I then noticed and remembered the handbrake, which was still tightly on.

A few days later, I was going to a Young Farmers meeting, and offered a lift to a friend who had until now, driven me around on a regular basis. The meeting was in the evening and I set off to collect Linda. I had worked out where the lights were and remembered that I should dip them when approaching another car. I was pleased with my new vehicle and the independence it gave me, I felt more confident as a driver. I picked up Linda and we headed off along the country road that passed her farm. A car appeared in the opposite direction and I duly dipped my lights again. 'WHAT ARE YOU DOING?' screeched Linda, clinging to her seat. 'I'm dipping my lights, what's wrong?' 'No you're not, you're turning them off!' Well, that was something else I learned about the car that night, dipping the lights is much easier than turning them off each time a car approaches.

I was conscientious about looking after my new purchase, buying polish and special cleaning cloths. One morning, I thought I should check the oil and water. I opened the bonnet and unscrewed a lid and looked inside the container. There didn't seem to be any water, so I filled a milk bottle with water and poured it in. Still no sign of water. I added more, yet I couldn't see any water level. I thought I should check the instruction book and when I did, I discovered that I'd poured the water into the oil compartment. A little worried about this, I tried to see if there was any mention in the book about what to do but I could find nothing on accidentally pouring water into the oil. After some thought, I decided a little water couldn't do too much harm and I should take the car out for a drive to see if it still ran OK. I drove around Blairgowrie and after several miles there seemed to be no ill effect which set my mind at ease.

That evening, when I visited friends on a local farm, I happened to mention in the conversation about my mix up. I knew I had a problem when the room went deadly silent and several mouths fell open. After a great lecture about the damage I could have done, my friend's brother put his boiler suit on and changed the oil. It seems I was very lucky not to have wrecked the engine.

Soon, I was to start a day release class in Accounting. The classes were at a Dundee College and I thought I should drive there now I had the car. This was greeted by gasps of horror from my boss and the typist. 'You should wait until you've had more experience before tackling Dundee', they insisted. But of course I knew better, I would take great care, it was the only way I was going to get experience after all.

If I set off early, I could take my time and hopefully the road would not be too busy. It was 16 miles to Dundee and I never once went over 40mph. At certain points of the road, large queues would build up behind me but I was determined not to let anyone upset me into going too fast.

I arrived in Dundee and headed for the College which sat on a steep hill. I wasn't sure where to park so drove towards it. The road seemed almost vertical and as I arrived at the top there was a 'Give Way' on to a fairly busy road. Pulling on my handbrake I sat at the Give Way and looked in my mirror; the hill must have stretched down towards the city for what seemed like a mile. Several cars were behind me. I knew I had to be careful to engage the clutch before letting off the handbrake; otherwise I would roll back and hit the car sitting behind. I therefore ensured my foot was well off the clutch before letting go of the brake, but the car stalled. I started it again and waited for another opening in the traffic, and once again, I lifted my foot well off the clutch before letting the handbrake off, and once again, it stalled. I have no idea how many attempts I made to drive away, but eventually I looked in my mirror and was horrified to see the queue of traffic going down the entire length of the hill. There must have been at least 40 cars there. My blouse was clinging to me and I could feel the sweat on my forehead and my heart thumping. People had gathered on the pavement to watch and once again

I tried to move off but now my battery was showing signs that it was going flat. I had to make a decision - should I get out of the car and walk away? Fighting this temptation was very hard. I sat for a few minutes longer hoping someone would come to my rescue, but I was on my own. My panic had dulled the sound of the horns behind me. Then suddenly, once again, there was a clearing in the traffic and amazingly I was off. I didn't know where I was going, I just drove. Eventually I saw a large car park and drove into it, parked, dropped my head on the steering wheel and sat exhausted and shaken for half an hour. Once I'd recovered, I drove back towards the college and found another car park. I arrived two hours late for class. I could only hope that none of my new classmates had witnessed the morning's escapade and I never mentioned it to anyone at work.

On moving to Blairgowrie, I was quickly made to feel welcome by The Young Farmers' Club, although I think in part I was seen as a bemusement. The guys found it funny to drive me to events because as they drove through the country roads, they would aim to run over rabbits and I would squirm. On one occasion, after attending my first disco, we went back to one of the girl's homes for coffee. We had the house to ourselves as the parents were out. They decided to play a game and immediately chose me to be a participant. I was blindfolded, which worried me, being amongst people I didn't know well and there was also a guy in the group that I fancied. I tried to remain cool and casual but my nerves were obvious. I was placed in the middle of the floor with everyone sitting around, and then my hands were put on the shoulders of a guy but I wasn't told who it was only that a safety pin had been attached to him and it was my job to find it with the help of the others. They would shout out general directions. I was mortified at the thought. I didn't know who this was, what if it was him? Where would the safety pin be? My imagination ran away from me. I made a few feeble attempts to feel about his arms, but the shouts were to go lower and then I not only froze but I could feel a horrible heat rise to my head. I tried to stop it, but I started blushing brightly. Some of the group still shouted directions but others sounded awkward, and I could hear a few mumbled comments about stopping the game. Several voices tried to persuade me to continue but then someone took off my blindfold and the room looked and felt different. Another couple had a go but I couldn't bring myself to join in, even though I tried to make light of my abject failure to be any fun. Soon, several people left and the party was over. I knew I had put the dampers on it and probably wouldn't be invited back, but they were more generous than that and it wasn't long before I made good friends.

The Blairgowrie Young Farmers' Club was an active and busy group; there was a variety of meetings and social events most weeks. I became the secretary and enjoyed writing up the Minute books; large lined books with margins and sewn-in pages which prevented them being removed, they were bound in red vinyl and were in common use by clubs and businesses. Later, when computers became the norm, I typed Company minutes on the computer and then printed them out. As I discovered, this was much less secure, and the temptation to censor or alter minutes of meetings at later stages was often irresistible to businesses looking to hide or distort discussions.

13

Losing my foothold

At the height of the summer, everyone became involved in the berry picking in one way or another. My first experience of berry picking came soon after my arrival to Blairgowrie. I joined a few club members to pick berries on one of the member's farms. I gently picked and accumulated my berries in a red, plastic bucket tied around my waist, then took them to the trailer to be weighed. They were immediately squashed and the farmer explained we were picking berries for jam, and that they had to be pulped into buckets. It took a while before I made any significant money, but eventually it was both fun and profitable. Blairgowrie was surrounded by berry farms, every farm grew an area of berries, many had acres of them, mainly raspberries but also strawberries. There was a Smedley's canning factory in the town, which made jam and where most of the berries went. However, there were rumours of it closing down and it did a year later. In summer, the fields filled with pickers from the Glasgow area as well as local mothers and children. Fields were strewn with colourful plastic buckets and punnets. There were wooden trailers and decking holding weighing machines at the edges and corners of the fields. Pallets of punnets and crates of berries were everywhere. The taste of fresh fruit was on everyone's lips. Toddlers would be put in makeshift playpens made from tattie boxes, which were situated at the end of the berry drills. This allowed mothers to pick, knowing their babies were safely playing with others. Hands were ripped by the raspberry thorns and turned bright red with a mixture of blood and raspberry juice, but it was easy to get used to the prickly work. On a first pick, the crops would be heavy and reasonable money could be made; you didn't have to be a professional picker to make it worthwhile. At first, strawberries seemed an easier option as there were no thorns, but strawberry picking was back-breaking, so most people preferred the raspberries. It was also very social as you could pick down a drill with a friend on the other side: As long as you both picked at the same rate, you could keep each other company with plenty chat. There was a lot of laughter in the berry fields; a great deal of banter. However, even this summer pastime would soon end. Firstly, the Inland Revenue decided to tax the pickers, which put many off. Probably only a few earned enough to be taxed, but many of the people didn't like the intrusion of having to give their details to the farmers or the Revenue, they were generally mistrustful. The farmers didn't like to ask for the details either, knowing that most gave false names. Some farmers chose to pay an agreed amount of tax on behalf of the pickers as it made life simpler. Then, within a few more years, machinery was invented, which picked the fruit automatically. Finally, many berry farms went out of business as cheaper fruit came in from Europe. I moved to Blairgowrie towards the end of the abundant fruit era.

Having settled down well and enjoying my work and new friendships, I was pleased with this new life. However, I did feel a bit of an outsider. I tried hard to fit in, abandoning my bike and bright coloured clothing for jeans and trainers. Then sweatshirts became popular and everyone seemed to be wearing them. They never appealed to me but again, to fit it, I wore them. And although I looked the part, I didn't quite feel it. The young farmers had an endless number of meetings, covering a wide range of subjects from farm walks, stock judging to water divining (one of my favourites). I learned many new skills, or tried to, failing miserably at floral art, but learning how to make good jams and chutneys. It was a well-established organisation with groups across the country and every year they would organise an exchange visit with another group. I put my name down to participate in a club exchange the following summer. We exchanged with a Yorkshire club and about fifteen of us travelled down in various cars to be stabled out with members of the Thirsk Young Farmers. A friend and I joined the family of a girl member at her home. It was a beautiful farmhouse and the countryside around was superb, very much the James Herriot country I had read about as a teenager. It was the first book which had made me laugh out loud, so this was a special treat to be in his countryside. Our first meal was a Yorkshire pudding, it filled the entire plate and then the centre was packed with the best beef and gravy I'd ever tasted.

The visit had gone well and on the day we departed, we agreed to travel in convoy back home on the A1. Just before we set off, a Thirsk member suggested that as a final treat, we could visit Lightwater Valley, a leisure park nearby. Two of the group didn't want to go so set off home on their own. The rest of us followed a Thirsk member to Lightwater Valley. The sun was shining and we had a great time on numerous roller coaster rides. Finally, a few went to look around the shops and the rest of us moved over to the rowing lake and hired two small rowing boats. Each group took a boat and paddled towards the centre. It was a sunny afternoon, but there weren't many boats on the large lake. We were boisterous and splashed water at each other; attracting raised eyebrows from other boats, but it seemed harmless fun at the time – the boats pulled close and someone in our boat stood up. Our boat then tipped over and as everyone fell in, the boat itself sank below. We had landed in the water laughing, then immediately began to swim to the edge. One of the Yorkshire guys swam towards me and asked, 'can you swim OK.?' I smiled, 'no problem', and kept going. I hadn't considered that perhaps some of the group couldn't swim. I pulled myself out to the banking and then realised there was something wrong - a friend stood on the edge shouting to the others - I looked around and saw a head go below the water. People began to gather around and I sat dripping wet watching an horrific event unfold. One of our group, David, dived in towards two people under the water, when they reappeared, David and Andy were holding Kenneth, then they all sank below again, then reappeared and Kenneth looked straight across at me, his eyes were open but there was a look of terror in them. I did nothing, I sat watching along with so many others in a daze of silence. When they appeared again, I thought, 'he's OK', but then they disappeared yet again. It now seemed the only noise came from a small fun train filled with people as it chuntered around the brow of the hill that surrounded the water. I could see the faces on the train looking towards us. The train kept going and I found myself obsessing about why it wasn't stopping – 'it should stop, why does it keep going?'. Another friend who'd swam to the banking with me, hadn't realised immediately that there was a problem and thought the guys were messing around. She laughed and started to take pictures before realising the full horror. Eventually Kenneth was pulled on to the banking opposite, and the little train passed by once again, this time it was slower and there was a dearth of voices. Then suddenly it stopped and someone jumped from it and ran down the banking to where Kenneth lay. I felt sure he would be all right; he was a fit and sturdy young man and was now surrounded by people helping, I could see someone doing CPR. I was so sure nothing could change this quickly, someone can't be sitting beside you in a boat one minute laughing and joking and then be dead the next.

The policeman wrote as I spoke, and then asked me to sign my statement. I have no idea what I said. I was sent to see a doctor and can't remember why. I know I didn't want to accept that Kenneth was dead. Everyone liked him; quite shy, easy going and he was always involved in the many activities of the group. The picture I have of Kenneth, rigid and staring out towards me that day remains. There were many associated horrors: Going to find his sister from the shopping area. She was deaf and not only close to Kenneth, but reliant on him to help her with the family farm. Someone ran to her as she appeared walking towards us. The image of her puzzled but relaxed face as she came close, unaware of the news we were about to give is haunting.

The loss of Kenneth and all its repercussions; the travelling home, seeing the families, travelling back to Yorkshire a few weeks later to attend the Fatal Accident Enquiry, all changed my life. These days they have a name for the after effects of such events -

Post Traumatic Stress. There was no name given to our emotions we were expected to pull ourselves together and get on with the life we still had.

The way we coped at first was by going around to each other's houses as often as we could and just talking. But then a friend's mother stopped me in the street and gave me a lecture, 'you should stop meeting up and feeling sorry for yourselves…think of Kenneth's parents'. She didn't seem to realise that it was because we were thinking about Kenneth and his family that we needed to be around each other. But the meetings stopped.

I wished I could have been close to my own family then. I found work pointless; I sat at my desk and looked at the accounts wondering why I was here and doing this?. I had been so career motivated up until then, now ambition seemed futile. A few weeks later, I left the accountants to return to my original career as a Farm Secretary. I also decided to become freelance, which was the one area of Farm Secretarial work I said I would hate to do, but more importantly, I decided to get married and was married within the year to Andy who had been on the trip to Yorkshire and had tried to save Kenneth.

My boss Graham, though disappointed that I was leaving, understood and helped me with advise on setting up as a sole trader. He then paid me a week's extra wages when I left, which I wasn't expecting and it proved to be a big help in the first few weeks.

14

High heels and puddles

I was lucky to get my first client within a few weeks of deciding to set up as a freelance farm secretary. A friend I met through the Institute of Agricultural Secretaries was about to leave a job to get married and arranged the interview. The farm was probably one of the most modern and largest farms in Fife, so this client alone would give me enough income to keep me going whilst I looked for other business. I put an advert in the local paper; the Dundee Courier & Advertiser. Job adverts were still printed on the front page with news inside. My little box advert read, Cameron Farm Secretarial Services: a mobile bookkeeping and secretarial service for farmers. It was exciting to see it printed but there was no rush of phone calls in response.

The Fife farm office was large and organised and I was in awe of the farmer: he was hugely energetic, clever and ambitious for his business. There were several farms in the business and part of my job was to drive around the various farms and collect delivery notes and paperwork relating to the fruit and vegetables grown. This was a nice way to meet others who worked on the farms. This was the largest fruit and vegetable enterprise in Fife and probably Scotland. As well as keeping the big red cashbook up-to-date, I was responsible for completing a detailed budget and cash flow. The budget for twelve months was written on a large desk-sized piece of paper, that was rolled up for storage. The budget was broken down into detailed income and expenditure for each month and then at the end of each month, once I had reconciled the bank statements to the cash books, I entered the actual figures below the budgeted figures. I then had to write in black pen any improvement on the budget, and in red pen, anything to the detriment. It was an impressive piece of work, which I enjoyed. I also loved to listen to the telephone conversations as the farmer made business deals. He had so much energy and enthusiasm that it was impossible not to be impressed and also affected by it. Andrew travelled a great deal with his work; he was on the National Farmers Union, Soft Fruit and Vegetable Committee, an important job because of the impact of European imports on the prices of Scottish soft fruit and vegetables.

During the 'berry season', I would go to the bank and collect money to pay the berry pickers. I would drive my rusty mini estate to the front door of the bank in Cupar, then go in with the cheque.

I'd telephoned a detailed breakdown of the change required beforehand, to allow them to prepare the bags of cash for my arrival. The teller would then pass over upwards of twenty large bags of change, making up several hundred pounds. As we loaded each bag into the car, it would slowly drop lower and lower to the road. Surprisingly, I never had any incidents whilst delivering the money to the various farms for distribution. On a Friday, I would collect two days worth of wages to cover the weekend and had to drive with even more care, especially watching out for potholes. One bundle would be put in the office safe, before being locked by a key which had a large brown label on it with the word 'SAFE' written on it. I would then put the key in the top drawer of my boss's desk. I suggested to him that this was probably not the best place to keep the key, especially when he was away. He agreed, and we looked about the office for a suitable place to store it. In the end, we agreed to hang it behind a small aerial picture of the farm on the wall. I rang my boss's brother who would be looking after things that weekend and told him what we had done and all seemed well. However, on arriving at work on the Monday, Dan came into the office looking rather harassed and said he couldn't find the safe key at the weekend. I said, 'was it not behind the picture where I left it?' 'Oh, I forgot you said that'. Instead of ringing me to ask where the key was, he had gone around his friends and all the regular farm staff to borrow money and their bank cards; gone to all the cash points and withdrew as much cash as he could. Then he spent hours driving around petrol stations and shops to ask them to change the notes for coins, so that he could pay his berry pickers. We put the key back in the drawer that evening.

After a couple of weeks, I eventually had a call about my advert. I arranged to visit the farm the next day. It was near Edinburgh. Getting up early I prepared myself, taking time over my outfit and my makeup. I went over my list of qualifications for the job and made sure I had copies of all my certificates. I made a note of questions I would ask about the farming business and set off ready to impress.

I found the farm without too much trouble. The Farm House was large and impressive. I drove through the stone pillars and parked in the wide front drive, but as I stepped out of my little mini a voice made me jump: 'Could you move your car to the back of the house?' I looked around to see a large tweed-suited man standing at the main doorway; he came over without any introduction and pointed me in the direction of the farmyard.

It was not a good start. After finding the farmyard, the same man, still without introduction guided me into a dark sitting room, crowded with old furniture. We sat opposite each other on two large armchairs; he had the typical large red cash analysis book sitting beside him. I smiled and waited for his questions, having given up hope of any formal introduction. 'So, what do your parents do?' I was taken aback, and then presumed it was his way of making small talk to make me feel comfortable. I said my father was a Tanner and my mother worked for Ladbrokes, the bookmakers. He looked astonished, then asked where I came from. I told him. He sat back in his armchair and said, 'How can you possibly expect to be a farm secretary when you don't have a farming background?' I kept my composure and replied that that was why I had gone to college and I had learnt a lot. I offered my certificates but he dismissed them. I tried to point out that not only had I passed all my exams with distinctions but I'd also received the top student award in both years at college. I could tell the word 'college' held little sway with him. He was not interested, but instead started to tell me about his own business successes; how his pig had won top prize at the Highland Show, pointing to an enormous picture of a pig on the wall. How one of his cows had obtained a record sale price…he pointed to another picture showing a large black cow. Throughout, I sat wondering how to respond. Then he told me that his sons attended an expensive school and asked if anyone I worked for had children at Loretto? I had never heard of the school so I couldn't say. I did hear myself desperately trying to impress by saying that one of my clients (I didn't let on I only had one client) was the governor of another large public school. He wasn't impressed, he shook his head and said, 'Loretto is a much better school than that'. I was amazed, there was a hierarchy in Private schooling? The conversation moved on to the reason he was looking for a farm secretary. He informed me that he used a proper farm secretarial business from the borders that travelled the country in vans displaying their logo. He then recounted what he considered a terrible experience with his current farm secretary: he had explained to her that she should write 'esq.' after the names of Gentleman when addressing envelopes. The following week he was horrified to discover that she had then been stupid enough to write 'esq.' after the names on his employees wage envelopes. He had had to point out that it was only when writing to Gentlemen that 'esq'. was required. I thought to myself, this man doesn't know the definition of gentleman and certainly isn't one. I began to glance towards the door.

I had not come prepared for this – what had happened to the friendly farmer and his friendly cows? Why was I allowing this man to use me to boost his social ego? He led me to the door still clutching the cashbook which had never been opened. He assured me he would let me know of his decision. As I drove back across the Forth Bridge, I felt deflated and very small; I knew I wouldn't get the job. He was not interested in my qualifications, my experience or my willingness to do the work, only that I was nobody important. As I drove home, I was angry, not so much at him, but at myself. I should have objected to his questions and his derogatory statements, instead, I allowed him to get away with very bad manners, and in doing so had failed not only myself, but the next person he would speak to in such a way. I considered why I'd sat through this: it was because I needed the job that I allowed him to behave badly, just as I had allowed the garage owner to underpay me because I needed that work. There was a horrible reality sinking in to my 18 year old brain; it was money and not knowledge that gave people power over others. I realised that how I responded, would not have made any difference, because there would always be someone else in need of money that would put up with being trod on. He'd always be allowed to behave in such a way. He never did contact me to say I hadn't been given the job.

It was a long time before I parked at the front of another Farmhouse again; receiving many an odd look from a client as I appeared from the midst of their farmyards in high heels covered in mud, tights ripped by their friendly dogs and sometimes breathless by the long trek between yard and house. Yet I was still determined to dress in my own smart work style and not in the 'country uniform' of jeans and green wellies, which would have been so much more practical. It was going to be my way of hanging on to something of me.

I'd soon discover that I'd been particularly unlucky with that interview and that not all farmers were as badly mannered. Although, many farmers did attach an unexplained importance to car parking arrangements: Years later, I was offered a Directorship in a farming company with the additional bonus that if I accepted, I could have my own parking place. This would have been in a farmyard which had no end of options to park. By then, I was much more secure in my own ideas and politely turned down the offer.

Despite this bad start, I soon became lucky in my hunt for clients, applying for vacancies which were advertised in the paper. Firstly, there was the Hill Sheep Farmer who took so long to make up his mind that I was sure he'd given the job to someone else until out of the blue, one evening, he rang and said he'd had a think about it and wanted to hire me. Then there was the farmer's wife who advertised for someone to help with the books for six weeks and I remained with her for three years.

I had to supplement my farm secretarial work with other work. A local hotel took me on as their bookkeeper and then I obtained a job with a Dundee builder's firm as a typist, one day a week. My work became varied and interesting; the people I worked for made it so. These pleasant experiences more than wiped out my initial bad one.

15

Stepping over the threshold

I had been told to 'just go in' as the occupier never answers the door, but this didn't seem right to me. I couldn't walk into a stranger's house without knocking, even though as a child, I had been used to seeing our key left in the outside lock to enable people to come and go. But this wasn't a council estate where you knew and trusted everyone, this was a mansion house in the middle of the country, so knock I did and then waited. I looked around me; the large imposing house stood on its own overlooking the Fife countryside, the house looked a bit neglected, the chipped, grey harling reminded me of home but that was the only familiarity. I knocked again, and then after several attempts, hesitantly, tried the large blue door and it opened, stiffly. I shouted a nervous, 'Hello', and then heard voices to my right, so walked down a dark corridor towards them.

Three people sat around a large wooden table holding on to mugs; a young man, an elderly woman and another lady. They turned to look at me and seemed to show a little surprise. 'I was looking for Mr Higgin-Botham, I've come to do typing'. I spoke as calmly as possible under the circumstances and fought the temptation to turn and run. Clover, my friend who was also a freelance Farm Secretary, had asked if I could cover for her whilst she went on an extended holiday. I was pleased to get the extra work but I was now questioning her motives.

'Oh I'm not sure if my dad is in at the moment', said the young man, rising. 'I'll check the office'. He went down another narrower corridor and moments later returned with a very tall, slim father wearing a large smile and greeting me as if I was an old friend. His voice was particularly grand and upper class. I felt my lips clamping together, terrified I'd get the usual reaction and he would freeze on me.

But I shouldn't have worried, as I didn't need to speak, and if I had, he'd probably not have heard anything, as from that moment he did not stop talking. I followed him into a room with a typewriter and to my horror, a tape recorder. I always hated those things. He chattered about where to find paper, envelopes and…the computer. This was my first site of a desktop computer. How amazing, he was the proud owner of one of these new modern devices. His arms flew this way and that; he enthused about how super a secretary Clover was, then, as though he had just noticed me, he stood very still, looked at me, smiled and then vanished as quickly as he had appeared. I was left standing in the middle of the room in a daze.

Slowly, I began to notice my surroundings - there was the most amazing brilliant lime material draping a small sofa in the middle of the room, but what really made this sofa stand out was the roughly painted purple walls. The room was cluttered with other furniture; desks, chairs, tables and a bookcase. Along one wall were never-ending heaps of paper. Intermingled throughout and quite distinctive, stood bronze statues and small, vividly coloured paintings, which clung to the walls in a variety of angles. This was the opposite of a shiny house; in fact, I had no words to describe this one.

I turned towards the typewriter and noticed the beginnings of a very large cobweb, it started at the corner of the desk and like a little whisper, strung itself several feet across the room where it finally attached itself to a tiny glass door, which was just high enough to exit if you bent down. What was beyond the door was a mystery because tall, green, weed-like plants grew outside and almost reached the full height of the door. Just then, the room door opened and I recognised the elderly lady from the kitchen. 'Hello' she said, cheerily. 'I've brought you a cup of coffee, I'm Mrs Crane, I come in a couple of days a week to do the cleaning'. I smiled, then wondered when the gardener would appear.

When Mr Higgin-Botham finally reappeared he sat at his computer and worked away quietly in front of the black and green screen. I typed in silence, working from the tape and handwritten letters. My job was to write to people who'd advertised their various businesses in the newspapers. He'd drawn a pen circle around those he was interested in and whom he thought might be interested in his insurance business, I suppose this was an early form of 'cold calling' but a more discriminatory 'cold lettering'. Then there was a flurry of great excitement, 'watch, watch…' he said, and with purpose pressed a button on the computer keypad. A rather noisy printer came to life and from it poured a long sheet of labels with addresses on them. He was thrilled and I was most impressed, it would certainly save me typing out envelopes, which were always boring to do. I began to relax, although conversation was something we didn't master.

It was at this job I had my first encounter with Royalty. One misty, wet morning I arrived to find the office teaming with men in jodhpurs – most held drinks in their hands and chatted in their grand accents. I manoeuvred my way to the desk, seemingly unnoticed by the throng: They would move aside slightly as though letting the dog passed. I suppose I looked like a dog as I kept my head down and shuffled into my seat. Once settled, I began to hear some of the chat; they were discussing whether or not to go ahead with the 'match' in the rain. The consensus was that they should cancel as the rain was just too heavy; then the phone rang. 'Yes, yes, of course, yes'. As the phone receiver was placed down, the man who'd answered it, turned to the others and said 'Charles would like to go ahead'. 'Of course, it's drying up, we must go ahead'. There was a sudden exodus to the kitchen and beyond. A few moments later, Mr Higgin-Botham popped his head around the door and said, 'we're having a polo match with Prince Charles....if you'd like to come down and watch, you'd be welcome, you'll see us, down the hill on the left'. And at that he disappeared.

I thought about it for a while, continued with my work and then decided I'd like to take a look, so I drove my mini down the hill and found the field filled with cars and horses. There was no gate, no security, just a field in the middle of nowhere which had been turned into a suitable spot for a polo match. Prince Charles had made the correct decision as the weather had cleared. I pulled the car in beside the row of Range Rovers and other large vehicles, which surrounded the playing field. I remained in the car, feeling a little out of place. I didn't understand the rules but enjoyed seeing the rapid action of the men hurling poles around, dressed in white jodhpurs and sitting on beautiful, athletic horses. It seemed fun. Then, Prince Charles jumped off his horse and stood on the side line chatting and watching. He then began to wander in my direction and stood in front of my car, blocking my view of the match. I'm sure he hadn't noticed me sitting in the car as he was still chatting to another player. Then without turning or checking, he perched his white-jodhpured bottom on my bonnet. There was nothing for it but to either get out of the car or sit and look at his butt. I realised that my car was the only one low enough to provide a royal seat. I wondered if I should do something, like ask for his autograph or say hello, but I didn't, I just sat there until he moved and then I headed back to the office.

Many of my visits to this client were memorable. There was the time when there was heavy snow; I had worried about losing work and income through snow so had bought a set of snow chains. These chains were not easy to put on wheels, especially in cold and snowy conditions, so, I found a spare pair of wheels with tyres at the local scrap yard and put the chains on the spare wheels. It was much easier to change two wheels when necessary than to try and attach the chains in a blizzard. I put my chained wheels on the car and set off on the 30 mile trip from Perthshire to Fife. The car managed fine and I was relieved to find the driveway had been cleared. However, when I tried to open the door, it was locked. This was a shock, as it had never been locked before. I had to knock for some time before a rather bleary-eyed Mr Higgin-Botham appeared and looked amazed to see me. 'I can't believe you've driven through this, Hazel!' he said, with astonishment. Well, since I had driven through it, I did a bit of work before being sent away before it became dark. On another visit, I had to take my newly born son as I had no one to look after him. He was very good at sleeping after each feed, so I took him in his mosses basket and was all set to have a quiet day in the office. However, when I arrived, Mr Higgin-Botham informed me that he had booked a place on a computer course for me. I had to set off with the baby to a local town and be trained on the use of a computer. As I entered with my moses basket and said I'd have to stop in half an hour to do the babies feed, the faces of the office staff was a picture. However, I don't think I learned very much that day.

Although I enjoyed my new career, keeping mobile was my biggest headache. I became the Scottish Secretary for the Institute of Agricultural Secretaries; this kept me busy arranging meetings and writing to members. For one such meeting, I had to meet a girl in Perth then drive to Dumfriesshire. It must have been the worst thunderstorm I had experienced; the roads were like rivers and the lightening flashed frequently and viscously above me. I arrived in Perth and approached traffic lights on red, as they turned to green, I moved off slowly, then suddenly another car appeared from the opposite direction and clattered into my side. I was thrown across the road and my car hit the traffic lights with a bump. The other car seemed not too badly damaged, but the man emerged shouting and saying how stupid I was. In a state of shock, I stood in the pouring rain. The owner of a nearby shop shouted at me to come and stand inside his doorway, and then the police arrived, which caused me to burst into tears. The police put me in their van and drove me to the police station, where they offered me tea while they contacted Andy. The traffic lights remained at an angle for many years after as a reminder of that night. Sensibly, the lady I was supposed to meet had decided not to bother venturing out.

I now had to find another car quickly as that one was written off and I was only third party insurance. I didn't know how I was going to manage, so Andy swapped his racer bike and £150 to buy an old Ford Escort. It went well and the bodywork was good but the handbrake hardly worked. One day as I sat in a client's office, a friend of the farmer's wife arrived for coffee. As she entered I heard her voice ask loudly, 'Who's blue car is that in the side of the Range Rover?' My heart sank, please let me have heard wrong, but as I followed the family outside, there it was - squarely in the side of the Range Rover.

Fortunately, Andrew had a good sense of humour and found it quite funny, although when the bill for the repairs arrived, I think he perhaps wished he hadn't laughed as much. I offered to pay but he refused, so without telling him, I reduced my account for several months. This car proved to be one of our better cars - in hindsight.

We swapped it, although for years Andy insisted it was I who swapped it, for a Mini Estate - to try and save on Petrol. This mini proved to be a complete waste of money, it turned out there was very little of the original car still there, most of it had rusted away and it had been reconstructed with filler. The petrol pump took dislikes to working occasionally and I would have to get out, open the bonnet and give the pump a good shoogle before the car moved on again. This became such a chore that Andy tied a piece of wire to the pump, bored a hole in the front dashboard and then fed the wire through so that I could easily pull on it when the pump stopped working. This was a great success. Thereafter, whenever it stopped, I would give the wire a couple of tugs and the car would start again. However, even this method was fallible and I lost faith one morning as I approached the Tay road bridge: the car cut out and I tugged the wire, but this time it failed to start. Things became embarrassing and rather desperate when I realised I was causing a huge queue in the rush-hour traffic approaching the bridge tolls. Unfortunately, as I was already on the approaching ramp, there was nowhere for me to go. I had to abandon the car and find a telephone box. Luckily, the farm I was heading to had its own mechanic on site who was duly sent to my rescue. Despite this problem and with at least two engine changes, the car kept me in work for several months, but we knew it wouldn't see another MOT so, after a bit of anxiety, we agreed to take on Hire Purchase and buy a newer car. I was still in overdraft at the bank due to the loss of the first mini, so this meant I could not get another loan from the bank. The only option was an expensive HP. We bought a third mini but this time it was in better condition than our previous models and it proved reliable. Things improved as I found more work and some of it was local. We had moved house with Andy's work and now we both had reasonable incomes, we were able to save a little.

The car was going well and I'd had several months of normality. I attended Young Farmers' meetings once a week: I was treasurer which kept me busy in the evenings and my bookkeeping work was busy and enjoyable during the day. I loved driving to the various farms and offices because much of it was through some of the loveliest countryside in Scotland. Going to the Hill Sheep Farm was my favourite, as I had to drive through a couple of miles of forestry across one of Perthshire's beautiful hills, to eventually arrive at the farmhouse which sat at the edge of the forest. The forest itself was at its most spectacular in the autumn when every autumnal colour was splattered on trees on either side of the track. The track would be carpeted in the fallen leaves and as I reached the top of the forest, I was met by the most incredible view of the Glen, often with snow capped mountains in the distance. If I had time, I'd detour past a small lochlan near the top of the hill and take pictures. The view was superb at all times of year but I loved it most in winter when there was snow on the ground and the mountain tops. I would often stop the car and just sit for a few minutes to keep the picture of it in my head, then slowly drive down the other side of the hill at a snails pace trying to take in everything before arriving at the farmhouse. The tiny, whitewashed farmhouse was always cosy: it had a large stove in the kitchen and I was always given a welcome cup of tea. This farmer, being a hill sheep farmer, had to supplement his income through other work, and so he also worked as a ranger for the Forestry Commission. This meant he could rarely be at home during the day. I would therefore often visit him in the evenings making the drive all the more dramatic. He kept a box where he'd put all his receipts and correspondence ready for my visit. The easiest way to work was to spread them out across the sitting room floor and write up the cashbook once they were organised. Fraser had many stories to tell, especially about deer stalking and the sheep. I couldn't imagine being more content than at this time.

However, my continued bad driving would catch up with me again. The summer had given us a spell of dry, warm weather, and then one morning the roads had become wet from a heavy shower. I drove to work in my usual mode of over-active thinking about everything except my driving. About a mile from the farmhouse a pheasant flew out of a hedge towards me, I braked quickly and very hard, the mini skidded towards the banking and I kept braking, it then hit the banking but didn't stop, instead, with great ease, it rolled front forward down the hill. Luckily I was wearing my seat belt. I saw my handbag and its contents fly through the air and crash out of the windscreen. The mini rolled onto its roof then sideways onto its wheels to come to a halt looking back up the hill.

I undid my belt but I couldn't open the door so climbed out the front window, which no longer existed. The road had the contents of my handbag scattered across it. I stared at it for a minute and then lifted the farmer's chequebook, leaving everything else as it lay, before walking to the office a couple of miles further on.

When I arrived - chequebook in hand, I explained that I had had an accident with my car at the bottom of the hill - Andrew said he would go down and collect it and was I OK? 'Yes', I said sitting at my desk and beginning to open the mail. About five minutes later he rushed into the office, 'Is your head OK?' he queried. 'Yes' I'm fine I said 'but perhaps I better phone the garage to collect the car'. 'Don't you want to 'phone home?' 'No, I better not, I'll get a row'. I worked for about an hour before he finally persuaded me to go home. He drove me to Dundee where I caught a bus to Blairgowrie, then another which stopped about a mile from the house where I then walked the rough track home

The garage telephoned to say they had picked up the car, the voice on the other end asked, 'Was your head OK?' 'Yes' I said. In the evening I sheepishly reported the events to Andy. He surprised me by not being upset and arranged to go through to the garage the next evening.

When he returned he looked concerned and immediately came across the room looking at me carefully. 'Are you sure you're OK? Let me see your head'. Perhaps something did happen to my head but not that I'm aware of. However, on site of the car I understood their questioning. The entire roof of the mini had been lowered by about half its height, nobody knew how I had escaped unhurt.

The garage and the insurance company agreed to put a new body on the mini, I was happy with this but now my biggest problem was getting to work until the repair was complete. We had never disposed of the old mini estate, so it had to be resurrected. After a few visits around the scrap yards we managed to piece it back together again, it looked rather odd as the bonnet colour didn't match the rest of the car but it started and I just hoped it would last the month until my own car was ready.

This resurrected car finally came to rest one day as I drove through Cupar to work. At a give-way, I sat behind a Securicor van, which was stationary. Then it poked its nose out of the give-way and a I moved forward, but suddenly the van went into reverse and drove straight back into me. Several pieces of my car fell off - my driver side door had not been working for some time so I had to climb over the passenger seat and out the passenger door, where I was greeted by an angry Securicor man - 'Did you not see me?' he snarled. I was beginning to realise that no matter what happens in an accident, everyone always blames the other person - especially if it is a gullible looking woman. However, after a feeble attempt at defending myself, I shook my head and told him to go away. He drove off as I gathered up the pieces of my car, watched by the great and good of Cupar and then climbed back through the passenger seat into the driving seat and drove off. Arriving at work still a bit shaky, I slowed to park the car, pressed the brakes, which then failed and I hit the house wall with a crunch. Several more bits fell from the car and I decided I had to give up on it. I telephoned the local garage, a mechanic arrived and I bargained for £25. He gave me the money then towed away the car.

My own car was nearly ready but I was without transport for another week. I therefore had to find other ways of getting to work. It was a walk of about a mile down our dirt track road to catch a bus into Blairgowrie, where I could catch another bus to Dundee or Perth and mostly to Cupar where the farmers would arrange to have me picked up - needless to say I had to begin very early in the morning.

This particular morning was dark and drizzly, there

was a fine mist hanging in the air. It was chilly as I stumbled down the roadway, which only just coped with cars let alone high heel shoes but I persisted on wearing them. Eventually I arrived at the main road where I would catch the bus. I stood on the corner and waited a few minutes in a decidedly bad mood about my awkward travel arrangements - why did I ever want to be a farm secretary – a mobile one at that? The bus appeared in the distance, I relaxed as it approached, it was still dark and the mist had not moved. I thought I should make the driver aware that I was at the Bus Stop, he was probably not used to stopping for anyone here so early. I stretched out my arm and waved; the bus slowed, it drew up towards me, I prepared my money, it turned the corner then proceeded to speed up. I couldn't believe it, it must have seen me - I shouted and waved, I began to run after it but it drove on and I watched the red tail lights go out of my sight. I screamed but no-one could hear me, I looked to the verge, and began to kick at a poor hawthorn bush, I hit it, shouted, then hit it again, I stood for about five minutes dumbfounded before turning and stumbling my way back to the house.

I did manage to keep my work going until the car was fixed but a few days later more disaster followed: our washing machine was an automatic but wasn't plumbed in. This was an old farmhouse with large bath-type sinks, so the hose pipes were attached to the taps whenever it was in use. On this particular evening I put on a washing and went to bed. When I woke in the morning and descended the stairs, there was a strange sound. I was greeted at the bottom of the stairs by several inches of water; wading through to our living room - there, floating in the middle of the room was my briefcase complete with our cat sitting happily on top. Going into the kitchen, I saw the sink was blocked and water pouring from the washing machine pipes, overflowing the sinks and running throughout the house.

Things were bound to get better I thought to myself as I walked along the riverbank that weekend, everybody has spells of bad luck now and again. At least I had the serenity of the countryside around me; there were no houses or people near us. The old farmhouse was a listed building, (when we received the notification that it had been listed, I took it to the Estate owner who took one look, ripped it up and dumped it in the bin).

One day, not long after getting the car back from the garage, I was driving to work through Dundee and I smelt smoke. When I looked down, I saw smoke rising from the steering wheel. I was driving in busy traffic on one of Dundee's main roads but I just stopped the car and jumped out. The traffic managed to pass but I had to abandon the car and run to a nearby garage. The attendant ran back to the car with me and it was now full of smoke. He cut the wire from the battery, then helped me push the car to the garage and once more,

I had to find a bus home. It turned out something had gone wrong with the electrics and a new wiring loom was required. I was sure it must have been something to do with the major repair from the previous accident but the garage said it wasn't so I had to take them at their word. The following day, I gave up my job in Fife with the fruit and vegetable farmer, I couldn't ask him to collect me yet again. I knew it would make life difficult financially but I had been under pressure by many people who thought I did too much travelling. It now seemed obvious to agree with them. Andrew offered me time off instead but I thought it was time to take heed of the endless events working against me. I transferred the work over to a newly qualified secretary from the nearby college that I'd met at an Institute meeting.

16

Kicking up a fuss

We had to move house again, as Andy worked on farms and the houses came with the job, this was termed a 'tied' house. They had their advantage - we paid no rent and they were close to his work, but usually they were in a poor state of repair and there was no security of tenure; as soon as you left the job, you had to leave the house. Andy moved jobs three times in the first couple of years of our marriage which meant three house moves. This was hard work and emotionally draining, especially after I felt settled in a place and didn't want to leave.

We had began life in a small comfortable cottage, one of its main advantages being that it was surrounded by berry fields and each evening during the summer, I would take a dish and go to the back field to fill it with fruit for our supper. No raspberries have since tasted as good as that fruit. I spent a lot of time decorating the rooms and a joiner friend fitted kitchen units. It was beginning to feel like home when the farmer's wife fell out with Andy and he was asked to leave. I was in shock; we had the HP payments to meet and as well as the car, we'd bought a washing machine on HP. I made an appointment with a lawyer but he had little sympathy. 'You shouldn't buy things on HP unless you know you can pay them back'. It seemed losing a job unexpectedly deserved no sympathy. However, Andy visited a number of farms in the area that week looking for work and found another job quite quickly. I think this annoyed the farmer's wife and she wrote a long rambling letter to Andy to tell him that he had good points but he should be more respectful to her and her son. It was a revealing letter, showing she envied her husband's high regard for Andy and resented her son's inability on the farm. He didn't respond but took time to say goodbye to the farmer.

We moved into a much larger farmhouse and it had the word 'farmhouse' in the address. It sounded grand and I thought it would give me more status within the farming community. I went to our local printers and ordered 'Change of Address' cards which I could send to all my friends. The fact this particular Farmhouse was less of a house than a Hay barn was for this matter irrelevant. It hadn't been lived in for years and the gable end had a large open crack running down it. There was damp, dry rot, wood worm, mice and more creatures living inside than in the garden, but it was a 'Farmhouse' and once installed I invited several friends for a coffee morning - open sandwiches being the highlight, having hidden my attempt at profiteroles in the kitchen cupboard.

About eight friends arrived and I ushered them to the sitting room where they seated themselves on a mixture of chairs, which I had carefully positioned around the open fire. Kindly comments were made about the curtains etc. Then I went to the kitchen and made the tea and coffee; new coffee pot in hand, I entered the sitting room and tried not to show surprise at how eight people had now become a single huddled mass around the front of the fire. 'It's a lovely fire', someone said, 'Yes' I thought, pity it doesn't give off any heat.

They politely returned to their seats and we chatted about the curtains, the fire and the artistic sandwiches. We ate, and then very soon they all left. I knew I had failed to impress, this was to be my first and last attempt at acting the lady of the manor.

Despite the poor repair of the house, I loved living there. There was no heating apart from open fires in every room and after days of smelling burnt rubber, we discovered that the electricity was so old that a new transformer had to be put in. It seemed that the electrics inside the house were about to burst into flames. But it had a special atmosphere and a sense of history. It also gave me freedom. A large wild garden, barely divided from the countryside around with endless places to explore. One day, as I explored the nearby riverside, I found a swan looking very unwell. I bundled it into my arms, like a pile of washing, and managed to carry it home. It gave no resistance, hanging its beautiful neck over my arm. I lay it on a blanket in our old wooden porch before phoning the RSPCA. They didn't come to collect it but said it would most likely have lead poisoning left behind by fishermen on the Tay. It would probably die, which it did by the next morning. I dug a hole and buried it.

Yet this isolated location didn't stop the TV licence van appearing one night – I showed him the black and white TV and explained that we only received two stations (badly) and he realised that this was one job he shouldn't have pursued...but we still had to buy a Black and White licence, though he gave us a month's grace.

The surrounding countryside was my dream as it seemed I had it to myself. I could wander without interruption for miles in all directions. Once again I had to order a telephone. It took me weeks to persuade BT to agree to put a phone in: finally, they explained that it involved erecting eight telephone poles to bring a connection to me and they could only charge me the standard rate of £80. However, they relented, the poles were erected and I got my telephone. I walked constantly around the area especially by the river which passed nearby. I would try to scare the pheasants off in the opposite direction when I knew there was to be a shoot but their stupidity never ceased to amaze me: it seemed that no sooner was one saved from a gun than it would immediately dive under the nearest car wheel. I never hid my dislike of game shooting to my clients, and it never seemed to irk them when I told them what idiots I thought they were. I suppose people who shoot are used to others complaining to them, including, as I've heard on many occasions, their wives or children.

The house was very cold, but with open fires and access to a sawmill, we managed to keep warm. In the evenings we would place a large log on the bedroom fire before going to bed, allowing it to burn throughout the night. We'd wake to a warm glow in the morning. We took up wine making, gathering elder flower and berries from the lanes that surrounded us. We survived a very cold winter, though in the mornings, I had to put a small fan heater onto an extension lead and put it in the car to defrost it.

We had been married a year when I discovered I was pregnant. We were both surprised and wondered how it would affect our life. I was enjoying my work and we didn't know anyone who had children, they were something other people had. Well, I thought a baby would have little effect on me; it would just have to fit in with my life. During this time I had to take on extra work wherever I could find it, it was the early 80s and Margaret Thatcher was in power, inflation and interest rates were going through the roof and unemployment hit an all time high. Everyone was tightening their belts and although my fees didn't go up, petrol costs did.

To supplement my freelance work and start providing for a baby, I took work driving an ice cream van at weekends and delivering double-glazing leaflets. Driving the ice cream van brought back memories from my own childhood but I'd forgotten how loyal council house residents were to their usual ice cream vans. One evening, I drove off my assigned route to try a well-known housing scheme in Perth. I didn't stay long though, as no sooner had I turned on the musical bells, than a group of kids came out their closes and started throwing stones at the van. I lasted a few weeks but was sickly with my pregnancy - one day, an outraged man jumped from his car in a petrol station and started screaming at me for going to close to his bumper (his rather downtrodden looking wife sat in the passenger seat waving me away and trying to tell me not to reason with him). I drove off, parked the van, and then cried for half an hour before returning the van to its owners and handing in my notice. However, there was to be no immediate escape; they accepted my resignation but asked if I'd help them with their accounts problems. I duly went back to sort their bookwork one evening but came away without payment. They explained and I'd also seen how hard up they were. I now deeply regretted having voted Margaret Thatcher into power, however, I was not alone, much of Scotland thought the same. Then, one morning I woke to hear the news on the radio: we were at war with the Falklands. I was gripped by an awful feeling of doom for our futures. I thought about the new life I was about to bring into the world and wondered what kind of world it would be. It wasn't just that we were going to war, it was the delight in many people's faces that frightened me.

17

Baby booties

After the baby was born, I wanted to keep working and we decided to buy a house, even though having a mortgage had never been an ambition of mine. I used to go walking with my dad and his greyhounds, sometimes we would walk through the private housing estates and Dad would say, 'look at these people who are so desperate to own a house, they can't even afford to put a carpet down or put wallpaper on their walls. Their life is spent working to pay a mortgage'. I had been shocked to see that people, who appeared to have more money, didn't even have carpets. It coloured my opinion on the merits of mortgages and I decided early on that I'd only buy a house if I could do so outright. However, Andy was keen and he had a friend who was a builder who wanted to help, so we bought an old flat in Blairgowrie which required a lot of renovation. Andy's boss kindly spoke to the bank as a guarantor for our bridging loan whilst the house was being renovated and we were delighted when it was ready to move into.

Meanwhile, I had applied for and got yet another farming client. Friends and family were slightly aghast at this news: how was I going to cope with a baby and more work? However, it was my way of saying I didn't want to become a housewife, though this is what most of my female farming friends thought was the ultimate achievement.

When I went for the interview, the farmer told me his present secretary was leaving because she was having a baby - I thought, there is no chance of me getting this job when I tell him I'm expecting. However, eventually I found the courage to mention the fact and he did not seem bothered. He offered me the job before I left, starting the following week, and this did wonders for my confidence. The reaction to my pregnancy from all my other clients was similar, from 'Oh dear, that's in the middle of lambing time', to 'at least it's not in the berry season'. I had a good rapport with the wife of one of my client's and we would often have long conversations about the state of the nation and the uselessness of men. It got to the point the farmer avoided the office when I was in and after I left, he would ask his wife if we'd actually managed to get any work done. This lady's reaction to my pregnancy was quite different to that of the male farmers. She had three children herself: she just looked at me and said, 'Good Luck'.

Like most woman having their first baby, I knew little about childbirth. Unfortunately, I was not even slightly prepared for it. I was too busy working to find time to attend anti-natal classes but as the day drew nearer I thought I should attend at least one. A group of about eight pregnant ladies sat in a circle beside the nurse. 'Firstly, we will all introduce ourselves', she smiled, 'and give our expected delivery date'. The first lady introduced herself and gave her baby due date as July, then the next August, another was July, I wished I wasn't last, but eventually it was my turn 'I'm Hazel and my baby is due on Saturday'. There was a roar of laughter from the group, but the nurse wasn't laughing, she looked at me with such sympathy that I began to worry. During this group I met another Mum, Carol Ann, who became a life-long friend. We met up almost daily after our babies were born to swap stress stories and recipes and remind ourselves of a life we once had but which seemed a distant memory. We laughed a great deal; it kept us sane.

And as it turned out, the birth itself was traumatic. I had chosen to have the baby in the local cottage hospital, however, during labour the doctor suspected the cord was around the baby's neck and decided to transfer me to the maternity unit in Ninewells Hospital in Dundee. I had been in labour for about 20 hours and was exhausted by the time we reached Ninewells, not only exhausted but in shock - I lay thinking 'How can a world which sends men to the moon allow another human being to go through this?' Then an anaesthetist arrived and administered an epidural. That man became my first true hero.

I went back to work 10 days after the birth having told Andy that I would never have any more children. I bought a Moses basket from a local shop and Robbie travelled in it on the back seat of the mini. He always found it hard to go to sleep, but the car motion would settle him and that would allow me time to do a couple of hours work.

On one particular day, I had worked for several hours, finished the job and said my goodbyes to the farmer and his wife. As we stood at the door, Margaret smiled and said 'have you not forgotten something?' The baby - he was still sound asleep in his basket on the dining room table.

To the surprise and sometimes annoyance of many, I coped with the baby and work well initially. As Robbie got older, I realised I'd have to find a childminder. I found a lady whose husband was the Headmaster of a primary school which I believed showed they were trustworthy with children. We filled in all the necessary forms and agreed times and rates. However, I found it hard to cope on the first day I left Robbie with her. I sat at my desk and every time the telephone rang I waited to see if it was for me, but it never was. I wanted to telephone and ask if he was OK but at the same time, I didn't want it to look like I didn't trust her. The day dragged and I found it an amazing relief to go home and collect him. Needless to say he had been great, and if anything I was a little disappointed he hadn't missed me as much as I had missed him.

I had been sure the baby would just fit in with my life, he wasn't going to disrupt things, and it would be easy to carry on working – however, I hadn't considered my own emotions for this child: I was amazingly possessive of him and the love I felt was overwhelming. It was difficult to go to work and leave him with another person that couldn't possibly care about him as much as I did, but over time it became easier and eventually it became the norm.

It was probably just as well I kept working, Robbie was not an easy baby: he developed eczema at six weeks old and was very hard work because of this. I trailed between doctors and hospitals trying to find a reason for the eczema; the only response I received was endless prescriptions for a variety of creams. These helped short term but the eczema always returned and was usually worse than before. Some mornings I would find him lying in blood-covered sheets: he would have torn himself to pieces through the night. Seeing your baby covered in blood in a cot is not something you're prepared for in any anti-natal classes, but it's something you quickly learn to deal with as a mother. In the end, you just want to keep the world turning for your child no matter what. Within a couple of months of his birth, we moved to our newly refurbished house in Blairgowrie. The flat was on the main street and close to the centre. It had been refurbished beautifully and although small, with just one bedroom and a tiny sitting room, the kitchen was a reasonable size and for the first time, I was in a house with a fitted kitchen. When Robbie couldn't sleep in an evening, I would put him in his buggy and walk him in the cool night air to calm his skin, this seemed to give him great relief and I enjoyed wandering the empty streets of Blairgowrie late at night, though we must have looked an odd site to anyone who saw us. When he was about a year old, I began feeding him scrambled eggs but no sooner did he have a couple of spoonfuls when his face began swelling. I lifted him and ran to the children's clinic in a panic. The nurse bathed him in cool water and said she thought he had been stung.

This sudden swelling happened twice more before I made the connection between the egg and his reaction to it. Food allergies weren't common or even accepted in the early 80s, so the doctors wouldn't take me seriously; I knew by their responses that my views were being dismissed when they prescribed me yet more of the same creams. One dermatologist did say that it was in my imagination and there was no such thing as food allergies, his words of consolation were that most children with eczema were 'very clever'. I didn't feel consoled. Eventually, my GP agreed that I should keep him off eggs which I was doing anyway. His skin was so sensitive that wool or acrylic irritated it. I started hunting out cotton clothing: again this was not easy to find. There were specialist catalogues which sold all-cotton baby clothes but these were expensive. I found the most economical way was to order cotton wool from a local knitting shop and knit his clothes myself. A few months later, the shop, Mothercare, started selling their first sets of all cotton jumpers and hats, little red, blue and white striped outfits. I bought several sets, delighted at being able to buy something off the peg, which he could wear.

Then we had to move house again. Andy changed his job and it was necessary for us to live in a tied house once more. We decided to rent out our flat but then discovered this was not allowed by the building society. We had to get a letter from the farmer to prove that we could not live in it due to Andy's employment circumstances. There was lots of paperwork to complete, as mortgages were only given for your main place of residence. This rule requiring mortgage holders to live in the mortgaged house was about to be changed by Mrs Thatcher, and the results of that change would prove far ranging for house prices and the spread of individuals buying houses for investment rather than homes. Meanwhile we managed to get approval from the building society and we rented the house to my brother. The tied house we moved to was lovely, a single storey cottage which sat on its own overlooking a gentle green valley. It had central heating which I thought was wonderful; this was the first house we'd lived in with proper heating. It also had three good-sized bedrooms and a beautiful garden. I decorated Robbie's room first, just how I imagined a baby's room to be: bright wallpaper, soft carpet and heaps of soft toys. However, Robbie's eczema continued to get worse and then one day after picking him up from his childminder, I noticed he was not well. Sylvia had had a bad day with him and I took him straight to the doctor. The doctor thought he seemed a little wheezy and prescribed a syrup. I went home and made semolina and fruit for his dinner. About an hour later he was very ill: he lay on the sofa not wanting to be touched and hardly moving. We rang the doctor and he asked us to bring him to the cottage hospital. Immediately, on seeing him, the doctor told us to take him straight to hospital in Dundee. He was only 13 months old and I was terrified as I sat in the back of the car cradling him on my lap. Dundee was a good half hour away and we couldn't get there fast enough. When we arrived at the hospital he was immediately put on oxygen. Soon after he'd been examined we were told he was having a bad asthma attack and was very ill. They put him on a steroid drip and placed him in an oxygen tent - this brought back awful memories of my own childhood asthma. As a child I had spent many months (on one occasion a nine month spell) in hospitals because of asthma. Much of my education had been in hospitals and I'd spent many long weary days wishing to be anywhere but there. I felt devastated that my son was going to have to deal with many of the same problems.

I hardly left his side, sitting on a chair beside the cot and holding his tiny hand under the transparent tent.

Robbie recovered quickly and made an impression on everyone with his clear talking, which I didn't realise was unusual for a 13 month old baby. Once again, I brought up the subject of food allergy but yet again I wasn't taken seriously and any questions were quickly dismissed. It was not until Robbie was two and half, and I had taken him to a private homeopath that the doctors admitted he was highly allergic to many foods. Funnily enough it was also about this time that food allergies were being talked about on TV and in the papers: suddenly it became a topical issue. This was good as people were beginning to take them seriously, but in other ways it was bad because whenever I mentioned Robbie had food allergies, people thought I was joining in the latest fashion. 'You didn't get food allergies when we had kids, couldn't afford to be that fussy!' would be the response, either directly or indirectly by older parents and even complete strangers who knew nothing of us.

Working and looking after Robbie became more difficult but I am sure my work gave me a break from being a carer of an ill child. I was always more energetic when I was with him and perhaps the guilt which every working mother feels made me all the keener to make up to him when I was at home. When one nurse commented that she had never seen anyone put so much effort into caring for a baby with eczema.

I was shocked, I couldn't imagine not doing it. Was it not normal for all mothers to make such an effort?

When Robbie was 10 months old I discovered I was pregnant again, we had planned to have another baby so the fact I was having one a bit earlier than planned did not upset me. However, because of Robbie's condition, I did a lot of research into the causes of Eczema and Asthma: I joined the National Eczema Society and the Asthma Society and obtained literature on both from libraries and magazines. I came to the conclusion the only way to give this next baby a chance of being Eczema and Asthma free was to give up my work to ensure I could exclusively breast feed whilst being on a special diet myself. I was sad about leaving work but all my clients understood my reason and were generous when I left the week before Rory was due. Several gave me lovely 'going away' gifts. A goblet engraved with a stag from the farmer who also worked as a Forest Ranger and a small bottle of Channel perfume from another. I was so thrilled with the expensive perfume that I displayed it on my dressing table where it managed to remain for a week. Then a friend visited with her toddler and he not only discovered the perfume but poured it all over himself. In later life he became a footballer.

The farm secretary that I'd covered for in the past was looking for more work and agreed to take over some of my clients. We arranged that I'd go along with her on the first visit to introduce everyone. Taking separate cars, I drove ahead whilst she followed on. The weather had been very dry and we were heading to my favourite hill-sheep farm. I drove at my usual pace through the forest tracks towards the top of the hill, enjoying the scenery around me. As I reached the top and my favourite view, I stopped the car to give Clover a chance to enjoy the scenery. I stepped out of the car and looked behind me: all I could see was a large cloud of brown dust. Then out of it appeared Clover's car, unrecognisable. She came to a stop and emerged amazed and out of puff as though she had just ran up the hill herself. She didn't quite appreciate the view as I had expected. I sheepishly returned to my car and led the way down the hill to the farmhouse.

I felt better about giving up work when I knew all my clients had managed to find someone to take over from me. Now I could concentrate on being a mother. Rory's birth was wonderful and by now the doctors had come to respect my understanding of Robbie's condition and the care he needed. I went to the Registrar to register Rory's birth. I'd enjoyed registering Robbie's birth as I watched the old gentleman carefully write out the details in a grand book with a fountain pen. His writing was beautiful and he took great care over every letter. Now, here I was registering my second child in the Blairgowrie register. Just as he finished entering the details, he gave a howl. I didn't move; what could be wrong? He put his head in his hands and said 'this is wrong, you're not supposed to be here'. I felt his pain but didn't understand. He now looked at me in fury, 'Your address, you should have him registered in Coupar Angus. I will have to put a correction through and you will have to go there and register the birth again'. I felt incredibly bad for him and also rather ashamed that I'd been responsible for messing up his beautiful book. I watched as he took a ruler and began drawing lines through Rory's details and remembered my upset at seeing neat cashbooks with corrections. There was little I could do but offer a pathetic apology and leave. I imagine he was one of the last Registrars to enter details by hand before being replaced by computers.

Being at home with two small babies and the shortage of sleep, was very tiring, I found these early baby days difficult. Then, one evening Andy came in and announced that he'd handed in his notice at work: He wanted to become a woodcutter. I'd had no indication that he was planning to leave so it came as a shock. In the days after, I began to suffer panic attacks, at first I had no idea what was wrong, I thought I had epilepsy but on having one during a consultation with my doctor, he told me it was just a panic attack. I was shocked that the mind could manifest itself in such a physical way and decided then not to allow it to happen again, and it didn't. We had to sell our flat to pay for the wood cutting equipment and we began to look for houses in North Perthshire where most of the forestry work was to be found.

18

Building stairways

I climbed the cold, stone stairs which spiralled around to reach the small, dark offices that sat above a branch of the Royal Bank of Scotland. After giving my name to a friendly lady in a cinema-style booth, she came out of its side door and then showed me directly into the lawyer's office. I was ushered to a seat in front of a large desk with its back to a window. The office was dimly lit and the furnishings were old, dark wood. Bookcases crammed with large books bound in maroon and gold, lined the walls as though they were wallpaper or part of the brickwork. The inevitable heaps of paper rose from the floor, corners curled and yellowed as though they'd never been moved since being dropped there. I sat opposite a small, greying man who seemed cheerier than you'd expect in such surroundings; definitely cheerier than I could be. Perhaps it was me who cheered him - a young, brightly dressed woman from another world. I handed over a paper folder containing property details of a flat Andy had visited the day before.

'We want to put in an offer on this house, can you do that for us, please?' The request was simple; I should be able to return to daylight quickly. He had a lined pad of paper laid out on the desk, a blank sheet waiting for instruction. He lifted his pen and started taking notes from the information I'd handed over, writing quickly with a fountain pen tinged with gold. 'How much would you like to offer?' '£500 over the asking price', I replied. He continued writing, glancing up occasionally. I sat in silence waiting for the next question. 'So, it's a nice house then?' 'Well, my husband says it is, I haven't seen it yet as I haven't had time. We have young kids and he's working away from home at the moment, so I have no car. That's why we're keen to move'. His response was immediate – he put his pen down, ripped the sheet he'd been writing on from the pad and tore it in half then quarters, and then dropped it in a bin next to him. I could think of nothing to say, this was not expected behaviour; we looked at each other. He then broke the silence, 'you will have to see it first' he leaned towards me, 'the woman must always see the house, it's the woman who has to live in a house. You'll be the one at home all day looking after children. I could not possibly put an offer in for a house when the woman hasn't seen it. The man, yes, but not the woman'.

I was a feminist, this was my chance to correct his assumptions and object to such small-town chauvinism: I had worked as well as my husband and would do so again. We were equals, and I trusted him. But instead of objecting, I heard myself agreeing, somehow it didn't seem a prejudiced point of view but an informed one. He spoke with concern more than power, yet power he had, and so I said nothing. Instead I found myself standing up and agreeing to make an appointment to see the house myself, despite it being quite a distance and a hassle for me to do so. When I told Andy he was surprised and a little frustrated by the delay. He, like me, was keen to move closer to his work and we didn't want to miss an opportunity, but we agreed that by the time we made an appointment with another lawyer, it would be just as quick to arrange to see the house. I organised a viewing for the next morning.

I was on my own with the children but found the address easily and the area seemed nice, quiet and picturesque. It was a large stone terraced building with a small stretch of garden at the front. I took the children from the car, walked up the path and pushed on the communal door which took me into a dark and dingy lobby. It was tidy but the stretch of stairs was a little daunting. As I climbed I realised that the house I was heading to was at the top, not easy with two small children, shopping and a buggy. I rang the bell and was met by a young woman who was currently renting the property. She welcomed me and I walked through a large hallway feeling my heart sink. The ceilings were twice the height of anything we'd lived in before, maybe even more. She took me through to the sitting room and there to, the walls stretched upwards towards high ornate covings. I wondered how we would keep these rooms warm? It was expensive keeping a small flat warm, this would be impossible, and decorating would be a major endeavour not something I could do. It definitely needed to be decorated, as every room was dowdy. Paying the mortgage was going to be tight, and we wouldn't have extra to pay for high heating bills and decoration. I began to realise quickly that this house would be more of a burden than a home. As I moved between the rooms, I also had the feeling the lady wasn't happy about the sale, I wondered if she was being forced out but felt it was intrusive to ask. Sensitive to the atmosphere of a house, I felt uncomfortable and before I said goodbye, I'd already decided we couldn't live there. I was now glad the lawyer had insisted I saw it.

Andy wasn't happy but accepted that I had to like the house too. Through his frustration and our need to access the cash tied up in the flat, we gave up on the idea of buying another house and found a nice cottage to rent nearby.

But this encounter with the lawyer had further ramifications: several years on, when my youngest child was in her first year of school, I was working in a farm office with the radio on when breaking news came through about a shooting of school children. The school was Dunblane, where that house was, and the school was where our children would have gone if we'd bought the house. Of course, I cannot know if we would have still lived there, or even had our daughter, but if we had, she could have been in that gym class. I left work and picked her up from school early along with many other mothers on that day, desperate to cuddle our children. It was only later that I thought of the link; how a small and seemingly minor action by a solicitor, Mr Hodge of Blairgowrie, could have changed my life and that of my entire family.

We moved to a rented house when Rory was six months old. Once again we were lucky to find a nice house in a small hamlet. Forneth village was also just outside Blairgowrie but our attempts at finding something nearer the woodcutting areas had failed so we'd agreed that Andy would work away from home during the week. Forneth was a row of nine houses, all different in size and style but of the typical grey stone and Scottish harling. There was also a joiner's yard and the owner lived in a bungalow in the centre of the village. Most of the residents were elderly and most of the houses were owned by the estate of the same name. The house faced south, overlooking the small Lunan valley and there was Clunie Loch just a mile away. We had a beautiful big garden and central heating which ran off a coal fire, however, once again no telephone. Despite this I was thrilled to move in. It felt like an idyllic spot with lots of places to walk and I discovered there was another young mother that I'd met a couple of times previously, also living in the village. Her son was the same age as Robbie and she was expecting another baby. Most of the other residents were elderly.

I enjoyed being a full-time mother for a while, taking the kids swimming, going on long walks and going to the berry fields in the summer where the kids played with other children whilst we mothers picked berries. We taught the kids to ride their bikes and had lots of chats over coffee and garden picnics where apple trees produced endless fruit and we thought our children would be small for ever. The church was involved in the community: there was a Young Wives Club, for people like me not attracted to the Women's Institute. It was similar though; organising talks and events and very much involved in baking and jam making. I joined with my neighbour, and when our husbands could babysit, we'd go along on the Tuesday evenings. There were regular talks from people who had travelled to exotic locations, they'd bring along slide projections and tell stories of their adventures. There was wine tasting evenings and beetle drives which included the children and raised funds for the group. Some were interesting and others sent me day dreaming, but it was a night out and the tea and cake afterwards was always worth waiting for. There was also a small hall nearby where local dances were held. The Tattie Ball was a particular favourite: held during the October fortnight (tattie holiday) which was originally created to allow school children to help harvest potatoes. However, the opportunities for this kind of work were becoming rare: most farms had started using potato harvesting machinery. These machines only required a handful of workers who would stand on the back of them and sort the potatoes as they were dug up by the machine. I worked on them a couple of times and it was certainly easier than the traditional harvesting where large numbers of people would dig the potatoes by hand and put them into plastic baskets before throwing them into a bogie. It was back-breaking work which I only tried once, and even then I didn't manage to complete a day: the farmer decided I was too slow and after a couple of drills, asked me to go to the kitchen and help work out the wages. That was a relief.

As I settled in Forneth, I still struggled to keep Robbie's eczema under control: it would get so bad at times that the nurse would come out and help me bandage his legs and arms. I depended on the Eczema Society for advice and they arranged for him to have a week away at an outdoor centre for children with severe asthma and eczema. It gave us both a break, as he was so itchy it made him irritable and grumpy for large parts of the day. I was very tired and also became bad tempered. Even hanging out the washing I was exhausted by the time I reached the clothes line. One day, I filled an orange tattie howking basket with newly washed nappies and trudged to the back garden to hang them on the line. Robbie was playing nearby and picked up the box of pegs which then spilled across the ground. I found myself shouting at him for being careless. 'Is this what children do to you?' I thought to myself. 'Where had this temper come from? Why was I always tired and why did walking just a few steps with a clothes basket exhaust me?'

I felt terrible guilt and wondered if going back to work might help. As the wet autumn arrived, I was unable to work in the garden and go for as many walks, I became bored. To fight these feelings I took up being a 'real housewife' with gusto: I knitted, and boy did I knit - jumpers for Andy, the boys and myself, then socks, then Arran knitting, every spare moment the pins were going. I looked for more and more difficult patterns. When I ran out of ideas and my thumb began to be painful, I took up sewing: this time trousers for the boys and dresses for me. One of the farmers Andy worked for had had new curtains made and there was left over material which he offered to me when he saw my sewing machine. I was delighted with the bright cotton green print and made myself a dress. Unfortunately, I didn't realise that it was Laura Ashley material and that the very distinctive pattern was popular with the farming community. I received many a strange look from farmer's wives who must have considered, or even had the material for curtains themselves. No one ever mentioned it though, and I only came to understand those looks with time and knowledge. Looking back, I realise that they were all 'in on the joke' and although I knew there was one I couldn't work it out. It was another 'green welly' moment but this time I was on the other side of the curtains.

I tried to take an interest in cooking but not very enthusiastically, I liked the pressure cooker and used it for most meals. In the summer I'd produced pots and pots of jam and chutney, everyone I knew was given jars of something pickled or boiled. Even the Health Visitor turned up one day with a bucket of berries. 'I didn't think you'd have time to pick fruit' she said: An incredible lady – she'd been a Health Visitor in the area all her life and was now working with babies of women she'd seen born. A spinster who'd seen so many fads come and go that it seemed her only true conviction on how to look after a baby was to ensure they were loved and given vitamins, she was a great advocate of vitamins and always reminded new mums that they should give their babies vitamin drops. Otherwise if young mums went to her with worries, she'd reassure them – saying that most problems pass with time and always had a similar tale to recount and reassure.

In the summer I'd taken up gardening with vigour, every vegetable I could think of was grown and I planted a beautiful array of flowers. I was amazed by my success in the garden and surprised at how much I enjoyed it. I wrote to a popular gardening magazine and received a cheque for £25 as the star letter, this was a lot of money and encouraged me to write more letters in the hope of bringing in extra money but it wasn't that easy. I also took up photography, taking photos of the kids, birds, the garden vegetables but always I returned to my first love of writing. I wrote short stories, poems and letters.

I'd meet up with my friend in the village most days. We took the children to toddler group and swimming, this was fun and made all the better by having a friend to share it with. The best tonic for any young mother must be another mother to share joys and problems. I can only imagine how lonely my life would have been if I'd not had my friend and good neighbours around me in the two years I spent in Forneth village.

When Rory was eight months old and being bottle fed with no signs of Eczema, I decided to try and find a few days work again. I was running out of ideas at home and Andy's work as a woodcutter was not bringing in enough money over the winter months. When I'd given up work to have Rory, one of my clients asked me to contact him when the children began school, if I was planning to go back to work. I wondered if he'd mind me contacting him after eight months instead of five years. I wrote a short note to let him know I was thinking of going back to work; a letter arrived shortly after to say he was pleased to hear from me and he thought his son, now running the farm, would be willing to give me a few days regular work. I was delighted, made contact and started the next month. My friend in the village agreed to look after the boys for a couple of afternoons, it was a little extra cash for her and the kids enjoyed being together. The farmer's son had been to university to study agriculture, so he had lots of new ideas and wanted to keep a budget as well as the everyday books. My big surprise was that he wanted to get rid of the ledgers and start using a computer. A couple of years before, at the start of the 80s, I'd been invited to see a computer at a firm of Perth Estate Agents, (these were agents who looked after country estates rather than the later kind which moved in from England to sell houses under Margaret Thatcher's Right to Buy legislation. Until then, there had been a legal requirement in Scotland for all conveyancing work to be carried out by Solicitors.) The computer was so large it had a glass room of its own and I stood looking in from the outside, wondering how much bigger they'd become. The room was to allow people to see it (there was a lot of prestige in having a computer) and to keep it in a safe, clean environment. It must have cost a great deal and I suspect they'd no sooner worked out how to use it when suddenly everything got smaller, and the desktop computer became an affordable item for many businesses.

Now, I was to be trained on the use of a desktop computer to prepare accounts. It was exciting and also a little worrying … perhaps once my client had the computer and could use it, then I would be out of a job. This worry was soon dispelled on the arrival of the computer, my work doubled and as the farmer didn't trust the computer, I was also asked to continue with the hand-written ledgers. This turned out to be a wise move, as the first system was an abject failure. When we produced the first Vat return there was clearly an error when the computer figure did not match the cashbook. The accountant was summoned and asked to investigate the problem. By the end of the day, I could see the accountant was using jargon to hide the fact that he had no idea what the computer was doing with the data. I then made the astonishing discovery, that not only did I understand what he was doing, but that I understood more than he did. To the farmer's credit, he did not give up and within a few months, after further research, another computer was purchased. This time the figures began to match the cash book and after a few months we took the brave decision to discontinue the hand-written ledgers. Then, we began the task of working out how to input a budget and run reports that were useful. I was not short of work and things seemed to be going well with the boys and my friend.

* * * *

Since I'd become a mother, I had had several doses of what I thought was flu as well as the general lack of energy. The bad bouts would hit me suddenly and so hard I couldn't get out of bed. However, when the flu episodes became more frequent, I went to the doctor. He checked for brucellosis as I'd drunk unpasturised milk on a friend's farm, but all was clear. He couldn't find any other explanation for the symptoms so I put it out of my mind.

Then, one evening at home, as I sat down to watch TV, I suddenly felt very unwell. By the time I reached my bed I had developed a severe fever and similar flu-like symptoms as before. The next morning I could not get out of bed, so asked Andy to stay at home to look after the children. He wasn't pleased but agreed as long as it was only for one day. I felt so bad I went to the doctor for an antibiotic and the next day, although not great, I'd improved and managed to do what was necessary to keep the boys fed and happy. Over the next few days I put the problem to the back of my mind again. It was winter, I needed to hack sticks for the fire, look after the children and Andy had to keep working for the money, I couldn't afford to be ill.

However, within the week I became extremely unwell again: I stood in our local Co-op at the checkout exhausted, all my energy was put in to keeping myself upright; my legs were like jelly and my brain seemed numb. On arriving home, I put the boys into their beds - protesting, and I went to my bed. The next day I managed to go to work but after an hour I knew I had to go home. I picked up the kids from my friend and went into the house, once again, I put Rory in his cot and Robbie to bed. I then went to bed and lay listening to Rory screaming; it was hard but I could hardly move and I knew he was at least safe in his cot even though completely miserable.

When Andy arrived home he telephoned the Doctor straight away, I told him I had a terrible pain in my side and asked for pain killers but after checking he didn't seem too concerned and gave me more antibiotics instead.

Within a couple of days I began to feel better but the pain in my chest remained. Then once again and suddenly, the pain became unbearable and I felt terrible. First thing Monday morning I drove to Blairgowrie to see the doctor - I do not know how I managed to drive without crashing the car because the pain was causing me to almost black-out. At times the road would become a hazy blur before me. The doctor sent me to the local cottage hospital for an x-ray and I managed to get home in one piece.

Then, I improved again although the pain was always there as a dull ache. A few days later, out of the blue and first thing in the morning, the doctor appeared at my door. I was pleased to see him and showed him in to the living room, offering a tea, whilst I smiled and told him how much better I felt. He looked serious and said 'you have pneumonia, you should be in hospital'. I was taken aback, I had heard of pneumonia but wasn't that something that old people caught? Anyway, I wasn't going into hospital as I felt much improved compared to the beginning of the week and who would look after the children?

The doctor eventually agreed not to send me to hospital, if I agreed to remain indoors and look after myself. I was happy with this arrangement thinking the worst was over. The weekend went well and when the doctor came to check the following Monday, I was fine.

The next morning I woke in agony - and there was no-one about. I managed to struggle my way to the kitchen and rang the doctor. By the time he arrived I no longer cared about going to hospital, in fact I didn't care too much about anything. I just wanted to get better. Lesley took the boys and an ambulance arrived. Andy was contacted and soon appeared at the hospital. I was admitted to a ward and after some hours, several doctors examined me but still I had been given no treatment. Then the consultant arrived; he took his stethoscope and listened intently to my chest, then brusquely asked me some questions as to why I was there. This surprised me as my doctor had written a letter and several x-rays had been taken on admission. Anyway, I told him I had pneumonia - 'Why do you think you have pneumonia?' was his next question. I was exhausted and my mind was not clear, his question made no sense to me. I thought to myself - I don't know, I'm here because my doctor said I had pneumonia, instead, I mumbled something about my x-ray. 'I'll look at that later', was his response as he pulled Andy to one side 'is she worried about the children or something else at home?' I was too ill or perhaps too shocked to be angry - he hadn't even looked at my x-ray, I wanted to go home. About half an hour later he returned, breezed over to me and said 'you do have a little pneumonia, it's not near your cyst, I'll give you some antibiotics; it's nothing to worry about'. A younger doctor that I'd seen on admission asked how I was. 'Can I have a painkiller?' I said, he seemed surprised that I hadn't yet had any and asked a nurse to administer them. I waited patiently but for some time no-one came near. When the nurse passed my bed, I asked her again. She replied that she hadn't forgotten but I knew by her attitude she was in no hurry to help me. Eventually the pain and the frustration got the better of me and I screamed as loud as I could 'I need a pain killer!' I was not popular but got the response I needed - the pain killers arrived. I was upset about being in hospital, away from my children just to be put on antibiotics, which I'd taken at home over two weeks ago. To make matters worse they made me feel sick. Within a couple of days, I knew I was getting worse, the pain had increased and my fevers became excessive and erratic. One evening, a lady doctor came to check on me and she was the first to show any real concern - she brought oxygen and sat beside me, and then I heard her tell the nurse she would call for help if I hadn't settled in ten minutes. I did settle but the next morning I told the nurse I was sure the pneumonia was worse - the consultant arrived in all his arrogance and pomposity, stood at the foot of my bed and said 'stop feeling sorry for yourself'.

After that I stopped talking; if I was asked how I was I said 'fine'. There was no fight in me, and as long as I had the pain killers, I coped. I lay in the bed for a further three days before another x-ray was taken. It was a Friday morning and I was supposed to see the doctor in the afternoon with the results. I couldn't wait, as I wanted to know if they proved I was right and I was worse, or if not, then at least I might get home. As the day wore on, there was no sign of a doctor, by early evening I could wait no longer and asked a nurse why I hadn't had my x-ray results? Her reply amazed me. 'I think the doctor has taken your x-rays to the consultant in Dundee for another opinion'. That evening he arrived, but this was a different man. Suddenly I had become interesting, he was joined by about six student doctors and informed them, not me, that I had pneumonia which had worsened and had to be hit hard with several antibiotics. Books were opened, drips arrived and mouths opened as he informed them of the strength of antibiotic which he would administer. His only comment directed to me was 'you'll be getting everything but the kitchen sink'. He seemed elated, a really ill person to treat, perhaps the treatment might not work, whatever, he was having fun.

It took me another week to get well enough to go home, I think they would have kept me in longer but I had had enough, the pneumonia wasn't completely cleared but I was now on tablets which could be taken at home. I never fully understood at this point what had happened, it seemed the cyst on my lung that had been there since childhood had become infected and then burst; each time it burst I would have the flu-like symptoms and then it would clear before becoming infected again. Anyway, other than a couple of check ups I thought that was the end of my problem.

The boys had been looked after by a friend. Rory was only 15 months old and when brought into the hospital to see me, he hid behind her legs, it must have been hard for him to understand why I had suddenly disappeared for more than a week and then reappeared in a strange place. it broke my heart and I cried for hours after they left. When I got home everyone left me in the house with the boys, Rory played in a corner for a few minutes then looked over to me - he ran across the room and gave me a huge hug, we all sat in a cuddle for a long time.

When I was in hospital there was a lady in the opposite bed, she had been having continual headaches. The consultant treated her like another neurotic woman and was often quite rude to her. He had no patience and his attitude was passed on to the nursing staff who would generally ignore her. I was the only one who would give her some time although I tried to limit this because she was under immense emotional stress which I didn't feel I could cope with. The shock came when she showed me a photo of her children, I asked who the lady in the photo was and she replied it was herself. The photo was of an attractive young woman and bore little resemblance to the lady beside me, yet it had only been taken a few years before. Her marriage was a mess and by her account her husband's treatment of her was horrendous - I wondered how people could do this to each other, destroy someone emotionally and physically. I felt a great deal of sympathy for this lady and was upset that the nursing staff seemed to collude with the consultant against her. I often wonder what happened to her and if she ever did get the help she needed. I resolved at that point that I would never allow a man to emotionally wreck me in that way.

After coming out of hospital I never had time to worry about my own health, Robbie's eczema and asthma was still causing a lot of worry; nights were broken and I would occasionally give him sedative syrup to allow us all to sleep. We had several more stays in the hospital that year because of his asthma and on one particular stay we had an argument with a young doctor over the treatment of his eczema. I wouldn't allow her to bandage him with coal tar bandages which we knew irritated his skin. This was a terrifying time as I'd been brought up to respect doctors, yet I knew that I had to speak up for my baby as he couldn't speak for himself. The clash between this doctor wanting to bandage him and me being steadfast in my refusal, continued for a couple of days.

I could see her chatting with other doctors and nurses at the main reception whilst looking towards me. Nurses would come in to the tiny end room where we sat alone and on dispensing his medicine would ask me when I'd last used the bandages, as though they were double checking my story, or apply his cream to comments of how sad it was to see a baby's skin so bad. Each evening I would drive home in tears, exhausted at having to withstand the pressure. Then things took a bizarre turn, the doctor came to the door of his room with another doctor and accused me of intentionally scratching his eczema to make it worse, 'she had seen me doing it'. I knew what she'd seen, so kept calm as I sat with Robbie on my lap next to his cot, his arm attached to a drip. I explained that I was rubbing his skin because it was itchy and the National Eczema Society encouraged parents to teach their children to rub rather than scratch as this caused less damage to the skin. I said 'think what it is like if you have an itch, it's impossible to ignore, so the best thing to do is rub, not scratch'. This set her in to a fury and she retorted that my son's eczema was the worst she'd ever seen. On hearing this, I was astonished and it had an immediate and profound affect on me. I knew then that I, as a medically uneducated mother, knew far more than she did as a doctor, and I knew then that I had been right to refuse her treatment. Robbie's skin, although bad, was probably the best it had been in a long time. The steroid treatment of his asthma had the helpful side effect of clearing his eczema, if this was the worst she'd seen, she knew very little about eczema. A few moments later a nurse came in to tell me that the doctor was now refusing to treat my son's asthma any further and another doctor would be given his case. I was shocked by this revelation, how could a doctor take her dislike of me out on the child? Another doctor arrived, a young handsome man who was very charming and showed interest in Robbie and his asthma. Then before long he was trying to sweet talk me into using the bandages. I gave in, I was exhausted, how could one solitary mother sitting in this white cubicle of a room in the midst of this weighty hospital keep up such a battle? I began to doubt what I believed. But then a flash of an idea came to me. I nodded my agreement but added that I would only allow them to use the bandages on Robbie with one condition - that they would take full responsibility for any bad reaction. The change in the doctor's expression was immediate and I knew he would not put the bandages on. Later that day he came back with the suggestion that they could ask the Dermatology department to take a look at Robbie. I was happy with this and a few hours later, several medical students arrived to investigate. To my delight, one of the students knew us, we'd met through the GP when he was doing his training and he immediately remembered Robbie. His first reaction was 'Gosh, his skin is looking great, so much better than when I last saw you!' When I told them about his bad reaction to the coal tar bandages, they said it wasn't a problem as there were other types of bandages which could be used. They then asked about his allergies to milk and eggs. During the conversation I mentioned that his lips also swelled when he drank diluting orange juice. One of young doctors seemed particularly interested in this; he suggested it might be the artificial additives and advised me to try to exclude all additives from his food. He explained about 'E' numbers on the ingredients - within a week Robbie's eczema almost completely cleared, it was a minor miracle for us all. Robbie was a changed child, he was now happy, his whining stopped and life became so much more relaxed, the extra work involved with the special diet we had to put him on was nothing compared to the work involved in caring for a child covered in eczema. The experience with that horrendous registrar had proved a blessing in disguise and it brought about a transformation in me – now I had more confidence to question people in the medical profession; they were human beings like the rest of us, not the Gods I'd previously thought they were.

* * * *

The following February I was knitting by the fire; it was around 8pm and I began to feel almost instantly unwell. Andy was going out and I mentioned to him I didn't feel too good, so I'd have an early night. A couple of hours later I was shivering with cold: I was worried as the symptoms were the same as before. I went to bed but lay awake, deteriorating rapidly, it was nearly 11pm before Andy arrived home; he took one look at me and called the doctor. By the time the doctor arrived, I was in a poor way. The young doctor kneeled beside me, 'Don't worry, you will be going to hospital'. I responded by repeating, almost like a mantra, 'I'll be all right in the morning', he held my hand and squeezed it tightly. I looked and saw fear in his eyes. The ambulance arrived and I was strapped into a wheelchair and once again, taken to Perth Hospital.

I woke the next morning in the hospital with a consultant standing over me. The previous doctor had retired and this man was now in charge. He at least spoke to me, but I found him patronising; 'why did you not have this cyst removed when you were 14? You were happy to go through plastic surgery to correct a pigeon chest, so why leave the cyst. That was very vain of you'. I was stunned by his comment, and too ill to argue: when I was nine, I'd been sent to a Glasgow hospital to have the lung cyst removed but I'd had an asthma attack the night before the operation and it was cancelled. Then, after many discussions with my mother, the doctors said it was too dangerous to go ahead and that instead, they'd keep an eye on it. That was when they arranged to x-ray me every two years. When I turned 14, I had an operation to have my pigeon chest corrected; I doubt I would have had any more say in things then, than I did now. The pigeon chest was a result of genetic problems or severe asthma, or perhaps both. Mine was certainly severe but I hadn't requested an operation to remove it, I wouldn't even have thought such a thing possible. My mother was very much of the generation who took her advice from Doctors, she put them on pedestals, so I'm sure she went on their advice on whether or not I should have the operation on my chest. It was a major procedure and rarely carried out, so I presume the doctors must have felt it necessary. It involved a cut across my chest below my breasts, then the breaking of my sternum and removal of misshaped cartilages. The operation itself was filmed and took several hours. The doctors were kind and went to great lengths to make the scar across my chest as tidy as possible. I felt more like an alien than someone who'd had surgery to improve her appearance. I'd certainly never considered that I'd had surgery out of vanity, whether a pigeon chest or a large, but tidy scar, both made me feel ugly. Now I was lying in a hospital bed with a severe chest infection being told I was vain and trying to make sense of it all.

I improved, but not completely and a decision was taken to send me to Edinburgh to have the cyst removed. The difference in attitude from the Edinburgh consultant was marked: He spoke to me as a person and explained everything. He understood about my children and my need to be away from them

for as short a time as possible. The operation was set
for six weeks ahead to give me time to arrange for
someone to look after the kids. However, this was a
huge worry, Andy could not afford to take any further
time off, and we were already behind with rent and
owed the bank over £1000. We had to find someone
to look after them for at least a fortnight. Somehow I
imagined friends or family would offer, but in reality it
was not practical for most of them. Two friends offered
but one had dogs and this would have been disastrous
for Robbie. The other, who'd helped previously,
was recently pregnant after having miscarried and I
could tell she was reluctant, so didn't impose further.
I thought someone would eventually step in but
looking back I can see the extra worry of looking after
Robbie was too great for most people, he was a big
responsibility to take on. As the time drew nearer for
my operation, I contacted the hospital and asked if
it could be postponed, but the consultant would not
agree, he said for my own sake, the operation had to
be as soon as possible. The Health visitor suggested
we place the children in temporary foster care whilst I
was in hospital. At first I was horrified by the prospect
but she let me think about it and eventually I agreed
to consider it. I expected that when people heard that
this was the only option, they would then step in. A
foster family was found who did not smoke, have pets
and were fairly close. We went to meet them and they
seemed lovely but I still worried over it. They told me

it would be a simple matter, like finding a baby sitter, so when I agreed and the Health Visitor arrived with a wad of official looking papers to be signed, I hesitated. She made light of it, said it was just formality and not to worry. I signed, but I was really anxious. When the day arrived to go to the hospital, we took the boys to the foster family on the way. I can't explain the failure I felt; it was as though I was betraying my children and had failed as a mother.

The hospital was an old Edwardian building but it had a friendly atmosphere and the staff were professional in comparison to the local hospital. I was in a ward, which in the main, was filled with cancer patients, and this made my worries seem much less. My room was shared with another lady and we quickly became friends; she was considerably older and was being treated for throat cancer. She would pour her heart out during the very long expanding days. It was difficult not to become close and I felt as though we would remain long-term friends. This always happened each time I was in hospital, however, people rarely do you keep in touch; once you 'get out' you don't want to hold on to that time, it becomes a different world, that was then and real life is now. You put it behind you, although I remember all my hospital companions with great fondness and clarity.

Another thing I had plenty of time for was reading, endless books and magazines. The evening before my operation I sat down to read one of the many magazines which lie around on chairs and trolleys and in people's lockers. I opened it at an article about a couple whose children had been adopted against their wishes, as I read further I became more and more concerned - this couple had put their children into temporary foster care whilst the mother recovered from Post Natal Depression. Then when the mother was well the Social Services said they could not have their children back. They had fought through courts and even gone to the European court, which eventually ruled in their favour, but it had taken so many years that the children had now been adopted and could not be returned. I was devastated - I had signed the forms, I had signed my children away. I went to the phone and rang my mum hardly able to talk for crying, she just kept saying, 'Everything will be all right, it won't be the same situation, don't pay attention to the article'. But what if I didn't come through the operation? I scrambled amongst my bedside cabinet and wrote a long letter to Andy: if anything happened to me he must never allow them to keep the children, he was to get them back straight away, stand outside their doors, cause a riot but whatever he did he must promise to get the children back. I never slept that night, now it was the turn of my friend to reassure and comfort me.

The next morning, I lay on the trolley numb from the night before, a nurse held my hand and made light conversation, we were waiting on the anaesthetist. 'Do you have any children?' She asked pleasantly. It was the wrong question; the tears started running down my face and I began to shake, not just my limbs but my whole body. The shaking became violent and the nurse shouted for help as she held me down tightly on the trolley. A doctor ran in to the room, ran out again and appeared back with a syringe, 'Just count backwards from 10'. he said, and then I was gone.

Wakening from the operation was a huge relief. I did not care about anything else; all I wanted now was to go home for the children. However, I hadn't been prepared to feel as bad as I did. I couldn't move, couldn't sit and could hardly talk for the first couple of days. They kept me in an intensive care ward and it was like watching some weird film of myself being looked after by others. The surgeon came to see me daily and when I was stronger he sat beside me to discuss the operation. It had gone well; unfortunately the cyst had become so badly infected over a long period of time - the first fevers had started three years before - that a lot of damage had been done to the surrounding lung and they had to remove about 75% of it. The actual cyst had only been the size of a 50p coin but the damage to the surrounding lung was too great. He said I had been very lucky and I knew what he meant; when I was first told about the cyst as a child in Glasgow, the doctor said I should have an x-ray taken every two years to ensure it never became infected, because if it did, it might burst and the infection could quickly travel in my bloodstream to my heart. I did take their advice and had x-rays taken at two yearly intervals until I was married: then my new GP had laughed when I asked him to arrange an x-ray. He said 'there are probably hundreds of people walking around with cysts on their lungs, and they don't get x-rays'. I felt silly and instantly forgot about both the x-rays and the cyst. Now this was the result of listening to a throw away comment by yet another poor doctor.

As my fortnight in hospital drew nearer its close, I reminded the doctor I expected to go home. He tried to persuade me to stay a little longer as some other problems had arisen and they were a little reluctant to release me. However, he could see my desperation and agreed that I could go home if they sent an ambulance the next week to bring me back for checks. I said 'don't worry about the ambulance, we've got a car'. I was allowed home on the 14th day and on the way, we stopped at the foster family and collected the boys. This was despite everyone's keenness for me to have a couple of days at home on my own without them. Nothing would have stopped me collecting them - they had had a wonderful time, it had been like a holiday to them, but I was very relieved to have them back.

My Health Visitor arranged for a home help to come in, Andy took a couple of days off and friends were very good. It was difficult to adjust at first, I was breathless and tired, even a short walk between rooms would exhaust me, I found it very frustrating. We drove back to the hospital the next week for my check up and I truly regret not having the ambulance. I can see and feel every inch of that drive yet, despite being surrounded in pillows; it was a nightmare journey and took me several days to recover.

A few months later I had an unexpected knock on my door and opened it to the husband of the lady I'd shared the hospital room with. He had two other ladies with him but not his wife. I invited them in for tea and he told me that Anne, his wife had died two weeks previously - the operation on her throat cancer hadn't worked but he wanted to thank me for my kindness in the hospital. I wish I had been older and more able to deal with that news; I was astonished that he'd driven over sixty miles to find and tell me this when we'd only known each other for a short time, but I was lost for words and we drank our tea awkwardly before they left.

* * * *

A few weeks after my operation, I saw an advertisement for a farm secretary at a local Estate in the paper, and immediately decided to apply. It wasn't full-time and sounded as though it would fit in with my other part-time work. Within a few days I received a call from the Estate owner. I explained that I'd had major surgery a few weeks back but that I was getting better and was sure that I would manage the job. The Estate owner offered to visit me at home for the interview, which I thought was very kind, so agreed. On the day of the interview, I remained in bed until about half an hour before he was due to arrive. I then dressed, put on make-up, tidied my hair and took extra pain killers. Andy helped me position various cushions on our settee to prop me into a reasonable sitting position without making it too obvious that I was far from well enough to travel to work.

The interview seemed to go well and as he left, he said, 'my farm manager may want to meet you'. I was happy with this and waved goodbye before going straight through to my bed and collapsing in agony. 'Did I seem OK?' I asked Andy. He thought it had gone well so I fell asleep. Shortly after, I was awoken abruptly by Andy shaking me: it was the middle of the afternoon and the farm manager had appeared without warning to meet me. I couldn't believe it, Andy had no choice but to tell him I was in bed. I tried to pull myself together and went through to meet him. He seemed nice and had lots of questions, all of which I found straightforward to answer, but I could tell he was concerned about my health. I assured him I would be fine by the time I was due to start the job, but felt I hadn't convinced him as he drove off. The owner telephoned the next day and enquired if I was sure my health would not cause problems; he was obviously concerned by the report from his manager. I reassured him and finally, and a little reluctantly, he offered me the work. Luckily, by the time I began, I was much better and became stronger daily. This was to be my first experience of an Estate Office rather than a farm office. It was a small Estate by comparison to others in Scotland but it was typical of Perthshire Estates. The owner was himself a Land Agent, so he was also the factor (the person in overall charge) – on larger Estates there are Factors who work for the owners and oversee the farm managers as well as other trades such as Foresters, Gamekeepers and Office Staff. The first thing I learned about Estates was their strong connection with the local community and how these communities keep an active interest in what is happening on the Estates. On the day I received the call to offer me the job, Andy's parents visited. His father walked in the door and said, 'I hear you are the new secretary of our local Estate?' I was astonished, 'How do you know that? I've just had the call a couple of hours ago!' 'Oh, it's all over the local factory, their current secretary is friendly with the bookkeeper in the factory and her sister works beside Aunt Jane…'.

Their current secretary had been with them more than 30 years. This was not unusual on Estates; people didn't seem to move jobs very often. I was expecting her to be sad to leave after such a length of time but she wasn't. I tried not to let her gloomy comments affect my enthusiasm. She worked a few days with me to show me how things were done – they kept a full double entry system and several large cashbooks were required. She spent time showing me where things were but I was eventually glad when she left me to find my own way.

I loved the little office, which sat in a small courtyard belonging to the main house. The house was only used occasionally but there was another flat across the courtyard where the Italian housekeeper lived. She was a typical Italian lady, big, outgoing and cheery and most of all she was a marvellous cook. It was her job to make me coffee mid-morning and she always brought it accompanied with a piece of her latest home-baked cake; I became addicted to lemon drizzle cake, although her other cakes were equally welcome. The office itself was small and filled on both sides with dark, grey metal, filing cabinets. I had a large, wooden table against a window looking out on the courtyard and under it was a very old black typewriter, which was no longer used. I coveted this typewriter so much that I brought it out at lunchtimes to type out opinion pieces and send them to newspapers for rejection. One piece I sent to the Scottish Farmer magazine, I was particularly proud of. I felt it was a brilliant idea, which should be discussed further. It hadn't been my own idea, but that of a farmer from the Black Isle: When visiting a friend for the weekend, I was invited to join a family gathering which included several farmers. During the meal there was animated discussion about the lack of tenanted farms available to young farmers (because farm subsidies were on the increase, larger estates were taking tenanted farms back 'in-hand' in order to claim the subsidies for themselves). One farmer suggested the best way to deal with it was to nationalise all land and let farmers rent their farms from the government. I had pondered this radical idea for some time and it seemed the most sensible suggestion I'd heard, I agreed that private ownership of our finite land resources did not make sense. At the time, I failed to see the irony of typing this piece on the redundant Estate typewriter. I was also naive enough to think the Scottish Farmer might actually publish it. However, I was delighted when I received a letter of rejection as most newspapers never responded, so I felt I'd actually achieved something and that someone somewhere had read my work. Then one day, I came in to work and the office had been cleared and redecorated and the typewriter was nowhere to be seen. The more modern electric one still sat on the desk beside the huge cash books. I wanted to ask but didn't, however, I felt I'd lost a friend.

The job was such a blessing financially, we owed a lot of money to the bank and now we were able to begin to pay it back. My lung operation had transformed me. I hadn't realised just how low I had been; putting my tiredness down to looking after the children. Now it was great to feel like my old self again and find energy which had been lost for so long. Like the first time I wore glasses, discovering how clear the world was, now I discovered how much I could do in a day without feeling exhausted.

My boss seemed delighted with my work as I updated procedures and began keeping a budget and preparing management accounts; the first time he'd ever had these and he found them very helpful. However, the manager seemed less enthusiastic. I discovered that grain hadn't been paid or trailer loads of potatoes were missing from payment slips. I was relentless in my questioning and chasing of funds; my first client, the fruit and vegetable farmer, had taught me a great deal about keeping track of produce and its payments. A local grain company which received all the grain had underpaid and I rang to ask about missing payments for seven tonnes of wheat. They said it wasn't possible as everything had been paid. They then sent a letter to explain that the tonnages wouldn't tie up with my figures because the grain dropped in weight after being dried. However, I had all the moisture percentages taken before and after drying, so was able to work out the weight loss and show that there was definitely an underpayment. A few days later the missing seven tonnes turned up – an oversight - and the money was paid over.

For about a year things went well, I took on more work and the boys went back to Robbie's original childminder. Life was very busy between work, playgroup, church and other social events but I loved being busy. However, Andy's work as a woodcutter never picked up; wood prices were low and machinery instead of woodcutters was being used more often. He decided to look for a job again and found one on a local farm with a tied house. It was in a lovely area –

Murthly - where we already had friends. We went to look at the house on a sunny evening and when we parked outside, I thought it looked nice, in a small row of other similar houses just outside the village. However, when we went in, my heart sank at the sight of the decoration and the floors. The previous occupiers must have had a dog or dogs, which hadn't been house trained and they must have smoked as the walls were filthy. So, here we were again, having not only the expense of moving house but also having to decorate the one we were going to move into, and I'd just finished the one we were leaving. I couldn't believe that once again there was no phone. I couldn't understand how people managed to live without a phone. For me this was the final straw: I'd already paid BT to install eight telephones in other people's houses, I was not going to do it again. I told Andy that I would only move if the Estate decorated the house and installed a phone. The next day they rang him to say the answer was a definite 'no'. He then asked if he could have the job without taking the house, but by now they must have thought we were the awkward couple and offered the job to someone else. I was relieved but Andy was disappointed.

Soon after this he found a full time job in Bridge of Earn, but it was some distance away from Forneth so we still had to move, and before Robbie started school. We also thought we should try to take the big leap and buy a house again, so we began to watch the property section in the local paper. The farmer that Andy was going to work for suggested a cottage, which he'd heard was coming on the market. We were invited to see it by the elderly tenant who planned to move into the village. We both loved it and wrote a letter to the owner to ask the selling price. However they replied that they'd handed it on to Perth Estate Agents to sell. I contacted the agents but they said it wasn't on the market yet. I asked them to let me know when it was. I wanted to stay in the country as we had always done. Andy suggested we buy an ex-council house but I wasn't keen, I'd been against the idea of selling off council houses, but he told me I was a snob and this hurt. Perhaps I was being snobbish. A few days later he arrived home with the picture of an ex-council house within our price range, which I agreed to go and see. The house was lovely inside and the housing estate was small and seemed pleasant with a large green area to the front. We were running out of time, Robbie was due to start school the next month, so we put in an offer which was accepted. We never did hear about the cottage and it was sold by the time we moved, although it was always hard to drive past it without wondering.

Fortunately, the foster mum who'd looked after the boys during my operation lived nearby and she offered to be our childminder; it seemed that things might work out. My own work was building up, several of my existing clients were requesting more time and I began doing work for a sheep breed society: This was a strange organisation, probably a bit like the Kennel Club. It had members and each member registered their individual sheep under a specific flock name. Details of each sheep were sent, noting special markings, pictures and parents. These animals were highly prized and many very valuable. I spent a great deal of time looking at photos of the rear ends of sheep.

Things didn't work out with the new house though. Within weeks of moving I knew I hated it. I could not get used to being surrounded by other people: no longer able to walk around the house in my nightie without making sure the curtains were closed; every time I went into the garden someone was there on the other side of the fence and everyone seemed to know what I was doing before I did. I felt claustrophobic and I had no idea where the boys were most of the time. They'd just go off to play with other children and I'd have to hunt for them. They fell out and began fighting with other kids and I became depressed. Then Robbie became unwell, his asthma flared and he was admitted to hospital several times, It was difficult to find a GP who was anything like the one from Blairgowrie and I had to take a lot of time off work to stay in hospital with him. The only way to cope was to free up some time, so the Estate job which was the furthest away, was the obvious one to go. They were sad to lose me and also slightly put out: they weren't used to staff leaving, people remained until they retired. However, they soon found a suitable lady and the transfer went smoothly. Then, within a month I lost the job with the sheep breed society, which moved south and suddenly I was looking for work again. I advertised and to my surprise, I received a quick response from a farm and agricultural manufacturing company just north of Blairgowrie. It was some distance away though in an area of Perthshire which I loved, so I knew I'd enjoy driving there.

Robbie was no sooner out of hospital than he was back in again, the doctors asked lots of questions trying to work out why his asthma had deteriorated so badly; it must be related to the house move. They thought the under floor blow-air central heating was causing him problems and we shouldn't use it. They also agreed that the double glazed windows might be a problem and we should try and leave them open. It was the excuse I needed to move; I didn't want to think about how to change things. I just wanted to sell, even though we had only been in the house three months and stood to lose money. The neighbours had been friendly but I never fitted in. One invited me to a 'China and Crystal' party. I had no idea what it was; I'd heard of Tupperware parties but this was new to me. With Andy's encouragement and my determination to try and 'fit in', I went along. The party was as it sounded: China cups and dishes and crystal bowls and ornaments. There was nothing offensive about it apart from the conversation. A room full of middle aged ladies talking about sex and telling smutty jokes was an eye opener, and a place I never thought I'd find myself. Should I try and laugh? Should I try and think of a smutty joke? I dredged my college memories but could come up with none. A much more attractive option: could I think of an excuse to leave? Could I sneak out? Maybe if I suddenly dropped a crystal ornament I would be asked to leave. I filled in the form and bought a set of expensive cups, which I didn't need, then left the party with new knowledge on perverted sex which I'd have preferred not to acquire.

One of my clients lived nearby and offered the rent of a cottage; it was such a relief to be in the country again. The cottage was small and required a bit of work, the kitchen was tiny, but the view was nice and it had a lovely garden. The area was peaceful and we had no near neighbours apart from an elderly lady next door, who seemed sweet and looked as though she'd only speak about the birds and bees of the natural world. Within a few weeks we had sold our house and moved to the cottage. The sun seemed to shine brightly that day.

19

The moments between...

I was generally managing to juggle work and children; I would finish my work at 3pm which gave me time to collect Robbie and some other children from school, deliver them to their homes and then collect Rory from the childminder. I wore a pager so that the school could contact me at short notice in case Robbie took unwell.

There were still a couple of jobs which I did on the occasional evening or weekend when either Andy kept the boys or I took them with me. I would take their wellies and before or after writing up the cash book, we would go out on the farm to see the animals. On one such occasion the sheep dog had just given birth to puppies. The boys were enthralled and then delighted when the farmer called the pups after them. On leaving we would be given eggs, pancakes or marmalade and on one occasion some homemade butter. I received a wide variety of farm produce from my many clients, potatoes, bags of cauliflowers and in the berry season buckets of raspberries or punnets of strawberries. Sometimes the gifts came as a surprise - on my first Christmas on an Estate the Laird's wife came into the office with a bottle of whisky and a carrier bag which she handed towards me. As I reached for the bag I jumped back with surprise, there were two small red feet dangling out of it. She laughed 'don't you like pheasant?' I hadn't tried it and wasn't really keen to either, eyeing the feet from a distance. She persuaded me to take it for a friend and on arriving home, I drove straight to Lesley's house and handed over the bag. She was delighted, 'a brace of pheasant!' I discovered that meant 'two'. I hadn't examined the bag that closely. Lesley cooked the birds and we were invited for dinner, I enjoyed it even though it was difficult to discard the image of the dangly feet.

On another occasion, I was handed a burger on a roll, 'you'll enjoy this; it's a lamb burger'. I did enjoy it, it was very tasty but as I ate, a discussion began between the farmer and his wife as to exactly which lamb it had been. I enjoyed meat but preferred it in disguise, if I put too much thought into its previous form it tended to put me off. As the discussion became more animated, the burger took on a new dimension, the image of the lamb would appear as I went to bite, it became harder and harder to swallow, I now had to appear interested in a conversation which I was trying to avoid, as well as eating a burger which would not go down. I'm sure I did a very good job of both as no particular notice was taken of my predicament and I was offered another, which I politely refused. The subject was eventually settled as to which lamb had been burgered, as the last piece slid down.

I built a good relationship with my clients, they had coped on their own whilst I was unwell, and a couple had attempted to write up the cashbooks themselves, which hadn't been a good idea. I returned to discover with horror, scores across several pages of my neatly written cash books. Others just kept everything until I could manage, which meant I went back to cardboard boxes full of invoices and endless cheque stubs that quite often had nothing written in them. It is almost impossible to remember what a cheque was written for after a couple of days, so to try and recall something which was written several weeks previously was impossible for them. Luckily, those were the days when cashed cheques were returned with the bank statements. I was therefore able to find out their purpose from that. In fact I often just wrote up the entire cashbook straight from the returned cheques. It was a long time before I felt on top of the work though.

As I'd discovered early on, this career did not only involve looking after a farmer's business accounts, but also looking after their personal accounts. Farming was not a separate business from home life; it was their way of life. This made the work matter more. I worried for them when prices were low or the weather was bad. I learnt to foresee their moods depending on the time of year and the weather. I knew never to ask too many questions at harvest time: 'How can I possibly estimate how much grain is in that heap!' Never to say, 'Isn't it nice weather?' in the middle of lambing, as it would surely bring on the rain and I only once ever said how much I liked the snow to a sheep farmer. One of my clients started trading in potato futures: this was a nerve wracking time. I would rise early and buy a paper before going to work in order to know what the atmosphere was likely to be in the office that day. Thousands of pounds were traded and either appeared or disappeared very quickly. It was a rollercoaster for all involved and I often saw a bit of competitive pride coming into play between the farmer and his friends who also traded –this determined a large part of the risk taking rather than reasoned thought. Although farmers mixed socially, they were rarely supportive of each other: more often they were being competitive, either to see who's crop was through the ground first, who started the harvest before anyone else in the district or who's beast got the highest price at market. They always told each other they were doing great, even when on the brink of bankruptcy.

A new piece of technology then allowed them to compare cropping standards to an even more detailed level. This was the introduction of tramlines. Until now, when sowing a crop, the whole field was seeded, but a new piece of computerised equipment had been introduced which allowed the tractor driver to switch off certain seed nozzles, thus leaving unsown 'tramlines' the width of the tractor tyres. This saved on seed and allowed more accurate spraying. The problem was, that many tractor men (and they were mostly men) were not always the people you'd choose to operate a computer. Tractor men tended to be the lads that hadn't done well at school, now they were being expected to operate in-cab computers. The other difficulty was that there was no way of knowing if they had worked the settings correctly at the time of sowing; they had to wait until the crop appeared. There was always a nervous few weeks between sowing and the emergence of the crop. When the fields began to turn green, every farmer would look on with glee if their neighbour had set the tramlines wrong and there were uneven, or excessive empty strips running through fields of barley and wheat. There were some comical examples, where settings had been changed mid field or the tramlines turned off completely part of the way through. None of this was funny for the hapless tractor men, many of whom were moved to other duties or retired early. Andy on the other hand, took to the new technology well and impressed his bosses. He seemed to be set for greater things.

I was in Nottingham visiting my Mum with the kids when Andy rang one night. Our childminder and now friend, was fostering a little girl who was just beautiful, and he felt very sorry for her. In fact, he felt so sorry that he wanted to adopt her. I was stunned. We had never discussed the idea of fostering or adopting a child, this was completely out of the blue. I said we'd discuss it when I got home but I was puzzled. In the end after meeting the little girl and talking it through with Andy, we made enquiries about the adoption process and before long we were going through the necessary and lengthy procedures. However, we were told that another family had been found for the child we hoped to adopt. We decided to continue, being now aware of the number of young children that needed a home. The process involved many meetings, psychological assessments and essay writing. We were finally passed for adoption after a year but within a few weeks I discovered I was pregnant. Everything was halted and instead of looking at children for adoption, we were allocated children for respite care. However, during the process of being vetted for adoption, we'd spent time analysing our feelings and our own experiences as children. For me, this meant dealing with many anxieties about growing up with an alcoholic father. Now, with new insight and more able to deal with past issues, lots of things changed for me: the main realisation was that I didn't want to continue with my life as it was and that any feelings I had for Andy, were now gone. Whether that was because of the endless difficulties of our early married years or that we'd just grown apart, I didn't know, but I knew we no longer had anything in common and wanted different things, not only for ourselves but for our children. However, I had no idea how to address this, especially as I was now pregnant again.

I'd begun working almost full time at a local estate office the previous year. Once again, I'd taken over from a secretary who'd been in the job for over 30 years. It must have been hard for her to leave, but she didn't show it; said she was glad to go and like the previous lady had little good to say about her work. She berated her boss for only giving her a mantle clock as a leaving gift, after all those years of loyalty. This did seem harsh…quite recently another of my clients had given his long-term tractor driver a substantial cheque on retirement, so a clock certainly seemed a bit mean. Her feelings about her retirement made its mark on me: I did not want to work for 30 years on low wages in one place expecting reward for my loyalty, only to be bitter on leaving. I didn't know what I wanted, but I knew it wasn't that.

The office itself was great, furnished with old, heavy furniture and a huge glass window looking out over fields and hills. They had a computer but weren't using it to its potential, so I made an impression with my technical knowledge. Once again, it was the son who was due to take over the running of the business and it was he who wanted to make better use of the computer. They also had a farm manager who seemed typical of most managers I'd known, straightforward, cheery, a bit chauvinistic and not keen on computers or accounting information. When I questioned several invoices for clutches on the same tractor, he tried to bamboozle me with mechanical facts, unaware I knew how an engine worked. He was bemused when he discovered that he couldn't pull the wool over my eyes and became more cautious.

It was typical of many Scottish Estates at that time; beginning to modernise but still retaining many of the 'auld ways'. Their gamekeepers still referred to them with a 'Mr' in front of their first name, so it was, 'is Mr David in?' or 'can I speak with Mr Peter?' I found it a strange form of address. I didn't like the sporting side of the Estates either, making my pleasure of poor weather on shooting days well known.

There was a peculiarity with farm wages; they were set by the Scottish Agricultural Wages Board which laid down the minimum pay for the different types of work and included an interesting list of tax-free 'perks', including things like dog allowances for shepherds. But also a daily milk allowance. Originally, this had come about because farms part-paid their workers in raw milk, but since 1983, legislation had made pasteurisation compulsory, therefore farmers bought in the milk instead and each employee, no matter the size of their family received several pints of milk per day. I found it astounding when I discovered that most of the families were receiving more milk than they could drink and just poured the excess down the sink. I suggested that it would be better for the families to receive the cash equivalent, as the estate was purchasing and paying for the milk to be delivered anyway. This seemed to be a revelation to the owner but a nuisance to the employees, who mostly were suspicious of change, and preferred to continue to pour away excess milk. Some of my suggestions were welcomed by both sides, others, such as keeping track of produce sold off the farm, were not received well by the employees. An estate secretary was very much in the middle, the buffer between boss and worker and it wasn't always the best place to be. I realised that nothing was as simple as I would have liked; the poor oppressed employee and the bad boss was rare, mostly it was a game of who could get one over on the other without the other noticing. Unfortunately, because I was in the middle, it was usually me who noticed. I had to draw my lines, and decided that anything that was dishonest would be brought to light but otherwise I let the games go ahead. This also applied to the games played by the farmers with the various government departments. I would not allow them to be dishonest but if there were grey areas where a subsidy claim could be made or reasonable tax avoided, I let it go.

There was a great deal of hypocrisy from farmers over their subsidies: they all received thousand of pounds in an ever increasing number of support fees every year. Although some were essential and necessary to keep a farm viable, such as the hill farms which existed on minimum income. The majority of subsidies were unnecessary and more politically motivated than about need. Most farmers could have lived with much less. Yet it was surprising how many believed they lived a hard life; they would often complain that their profit was lower than the average wage. I would point out that someone on the average wage had to pay their rent or mortgage, their car and fuel and heating from that wage, whilst they had none of this as these were considered business expenses. The farmer's profit was generally pocket money and often very good pocket money. However, I knew by now that everyone judged their financial state by looking at someone who had more and never less. The biggest problem with farming was that most of it was not in the control of the farmer. Such things as weather, Government policies and supermarkets made the decisions which affected their income. Very little depended on their ability to run a business, most were becoming employees of either the State or the Supermarkets and the knowledge of land management was being set aside in many ways.

To obtain the various subsidies, record keeping requirements were becoming stricter, and the recent surge in the use of PCs encouraged many of the younger generation to start looking at computerised accounting systems. I was lucky to be involved with computers at an early stage as I became more in demand to help with these new systems.

20

Fear of falling

Four days of uncontrollable crying had brought me to ask, 'Am I having a nervous breakdown?' I had heard of people having them but never knew what they actually were. Anyway, I had to do something to pull myself out of this very dark hole which I was sinking into. The children must be feeling the strain, the boys aged 9 and 7 said little to me, they knew something was wrong but never asked, I tried to keep the tears private in either the bathroom or my office. I'd pull myself together enough to take the boys to and from school, make dinner, and see them to bed but that was about all the contact I was having with them in these few days. Heather, my daughter at only 11 months was too young to notice; when she was awake she smiled and played with the boys, always enjoying a carry-on. I would look at her and feel such guilt that I would then begin to cry again. 'How could I be so miserable when I had such wonderful children?' It was only the realisation that the thing which was holding me together, the kids, was the thing I would end up losing if I did not do something about my depressed state. My solution, I'd find a hypnotist and ask them to erase memories of the previous year. Unfortunately, after paying £25, which I couldn't afford, I was told that although she could erase memories, it was unethical. Instead, I lay on a couch listening to dreamy music and pretending to be on a beach. It was rather pointless, although she did say I was suffering from a broken heart. This gave me something physical to concentrate on: something that was broken could be mended. I would mend myself.

I hadn't seen anyone over these days, a brief hello to other parents when I dropped the boys off to birthday parties. I had spoken to several people on the 'phone, my mother and my sister knew I was down but how could I tell them I thought I was going off my head? Andy and I had separated two months previously. Unusually, he'd been telephoning me every night over these last days: having been together for 11 years he must have sensed that something was very wrong. I didn't want to speak to him about it though, in fact if anything I found his telephone calls made things worse, reinforcing my sense of guilt. However, he was coming over to see the children, and this is why I had to pull myself together. I thought if he saw the state I was in, he might give up his job and take the children. I couldn't let that happen. He had already suggested we would get back together and I knew this too would give him an extra lever for that. I had no intention of going back but I wanted desperately to keep some form of reasonable relationship for the sake of the children.

I had to go to work in two days, sit in an office with a client for six hours, occasionally chat, concentrate on detailed accounts and pretend that I was coping. I had been with this client for many years, so he knew me well. When I had spoken to him for a brief moment on the telephone, I sensed he knew I wasn't coping. What does someone like that say to you under these circumstances? I suppose they try to be supportive, it is all they can do after all. He didn't know me well enough to ask personal questions but probably felt he knew me well enough to care. Eleven months before, I had given birth to Heather, she was born healthy and although the birth was not a good experience, I was well and allowed home within 48 hours. Throughout the pregnancy many people would say, 'You'll be hoping for a girl this time!' I was already very close to my sons therefore I never felt another boy would be a disappointment. At the five month scan, I asked the sex of the baby and was told it was to be a girl, then when people said that I would be hoping for a girl, I was able to say 'I'm not hoping for anything other than a healthy baby as I know the sex'.

Throughout my pregnancy I worried much more than before about the baby's health. I had been taking tablets for PMT and this therefore put a worry in my mind about the baby's wellbeing. The lady who worked for me had also become pregnant and I was trying to support her as she worried about her baby's health for different reasons. The thought that I had two healthy babies already and this time my luck might run out, was also there. I suppose all these thoughts must go through many pregnant mothers' minds.

When I first discovered I was pregnant, I was in the process of setting up a new business venture: training computerised accounts. The new business would develop what I'd been doing for the previous 10 years, but I would be using my experience to help farmers set up their accounts accurately on computer and train them and their secretaries to prepare management reports and budgets. I'd be doing less of the actual day to day bookkeeping work and concentrate more on the training and management accounts. A client had suggested the idea to me and there was definitely a niche in the market for such a business. I had been under a bit of stress and didn't sleep much, so when my period was a few days late I put it down to stress. I should have known better, I was never late, even through previous stress and illness, I was always on time but my mind was so full of work that I didn't consider I could be pregnant - we were being very careful about contraception. Andy got worried and said to me one Saturday morning that I should buy one of these home test kits. I was sceptical but to put his mind at rest, I said I would. My two boys and I trailed the chemists in Perth looking for a kit, I didn't want to ask, so if I couldn't see them on the shelve, I tried another chemist. Robbie my eldest son kept asking what I was looking for - nothing special, I would snap as I got fed up looking. I then asked them to stand outside a shop whilst I went in. I asked for a kit and handed over the £8 grudgingly. Even when I got home and went through the routine in the bathroom, I felt it was all a waste of time and money. I read the instructions carefully and then finally it said to put the drops of liquid into the urine collected, if after one minute it began to turn pink you were pregnant.

I put a few drops into the urine; a watch in my hand ready to time the minute: I couldn't believe my eyes - within seconds it began to turn not just pink but almost bright red. I stared, and then read the instructions again and stared at it again, and then I burst into tears - how? I couldn't understand. I now had to decide what to do, the adoption process was ongoing, and would I have to give up the idea of the business? However, Andy was keen that I carry on with the business; he said he would help and take extra time off when I had the baby. I had also just asked a friend to work for me part-time and she would be able to help out when the baby was born, I decided to go ahead with the business but we halted the idea of an adoption. Somehow, I had forgotten what it was really like when the boys were babies, the memories of those days were locked away in the back of my mind but they would soon come flooding back with a vengeance.

When I told my boys the next day, Robbie sighed relief and said, 'Oh is that what yesterday was all about then! '

Perhaps I needed a break. A friend invited me to London for the weekend, she was a member of the Scottish Fiddle Orchestra and they were performing in the Royal Albert Hall. Andy had agreed to keep the boys for the weekend. He'd just returned from a trip to France with the local pipe band. I was thrilled with the idea of visiting London and getting away from all my worries. On the day we were to leave, I rushed straight from work and picked up Aileen to catch the train from Perth to Glasgow. A special train from Glasgow Central Station had been laid on for the Orchestra. We'd allowed ourselves plenty of time. It was a relief to sit on the train and catch our breath; we could leave our problems at home for a couple of days. 'It's been so long since I've been on a train' I remarked. The train was one of the modern sleeker models, the carriages bright and pleasant inside. 'In fact, the last time I was on a train, it broke down', I joked. No sooner was the remark complete than the train pulled to a stop - I could feel several eyes in the carriage turn to me. I smiled. 'We can't have broken down' I reassured Aileen and the rest of the passengers, but indeed we had, only a few miles out of Perth. We chatted away but as the time passed we became more anxious about catching our train in Glasgow. When we eventually started moving again the guard assured us we would be on time. However, we had to get from Glasgow Queen Street to Glasgow Central in only five minutes - anyone who knows this route will know that the minimum it takes is about 4 minutes running at full speed, but we had heavy suitcases, a violin and lots of pedestrians in the way. Somehow we made it – just. We collapsed in our seats as the train moved away. It was not the best of starts to my relaxing weekend but the train journey made up for it, many of the orchestra played their fiddles and accordions as the train chuntered along. There was a great deal of liquid refreshment and I stood watching some beautiful countryside whiz past to the sound of terrific fiddle music. The train itself, which was an original clattery locomotive, with the wood panelling and draughty joins between carriages, hired from the railway preservation society, seemed to be part of the music too.

Our hotel was excellent, and on the Saturday morning Aileen went to rehearsal, so I encountered London by myself for only the second time in my life. I expected it to be very busy, but at 9am on a Saturday morning it was quieter than Perth. Everyone I met seemed to speak and I headed for the big shops with plenty of advice from people in the subway. There were lots of things to see before I headed for the Albert Hall to meet up with the orchestra after rehearsal. I eventually found it, after asking several people for directions and then battling my way through a protest march. We went straight back to the shops again and trailed until exhausted. In the evening we dressed up in our evening dresses ready for the concert. Aileen had to go ahead on the bus and I walked towards the Hall enjoying the atmosphere of a now very busy London. There was a long queue and my feet ached so I hoped we wouldn't have to wait too long, but we waited and waited. Then the police arrived: there had been an IRA bomb scare and we'd have to wait a bit longer. Eventually, the doors opened and everyone was relieved to sit down. The first half went well, however, at the interval it was announced there had been another bomb scare and we had to leave: the concert was cancelled. I felt desperately disappointed, my aching feet managed to walk me down the road until I found a Burger King and I sat down for a rest, eating something I didn't really want to eat, and getting odd looks from other customers because of my long dress. I should have known the minute the train broke down this was not going to be the break I'd hoped for.

Arriving home from the hospital with Heather, I was completely unprepared for the reaction of other people. I felt happy, but moreover relief, such great relief that my baby had after all been healthy. I'd prepared myself throughout the pregnancy for a handicapped child; even to the point of arranging to work from home whilst looking after the baby.

Now there was no need, my baby was well. The relief was tremendous - but friends, family and even just acquaintances were overjoyed. I had had a girl - the cards came flooding in, as did the gifts, it was overwhelming and I began to feel guilt, why didn't I feel as thrilled as they were that I'd had a girl? After all she was my baby - my daughter, why did I not feel this great joy everyone else was showing? I think I was frightened to be too happy as it seemed too perfect to everyone else who had no idea how I was feeling about my marriage. The guilt became so great I began to think I would be punished in some way, perhaps I would lose her to cot death. The feeling that something was bound to go wrong grew stronger, and I became obsessed by the worry of cot death and watched her constantly. If she was sleeping too still, I would poke her or lift her. I had read about other people doing this and I couldn't believe I was reacting in this way: Anne Diamond seemed to be constantly on the TV talking about her own recent loss. I realised I had to get back to work as that might help put things back in perspective. I mentioned my worry to couple of friends but they didn't realise how serious it was. The health visitor arrived one day as I was crying; I told her that Anne Diamond had just been on TV talking about cot death and it had upset me. She tried to reassure me and moved on to the subject of father's sometimes getting post-natal depression, which was mostly overlooked. My own problem was deeper.

Being self-employed I couldn't afford to take too much time off, with no maternity pay and the business not one year old, I had to keep working. I had employed a friend who was meant to cover for me after I'd had the baby, but she was now several months pregnant herself, so wasn't able to do as much as I'd hoped. I therefore went back to work a fortnight after Heather was born, after finding a lovely childminder, Senga.

Farming was experiencing many changes and many problems: the introduction of set-aside, the GATT talks and there was a general recession. However, this was good for my business, as more farmers wanted management information and budgets. I seemed to be coping, I had breast fed for six weeks, Heather's childminder was great and she had settled well, she was a good baby and for a few weeks everything began to improve. However, Andy had only managed one week off, he was promoted to Manager six months before and all his time was now taken up with his work. Our relationship during the pregnancy had completely disintegrated. I was tired and very sick, sometimes having to leave work at lunchtime as the nausea became too much. To help, I'd make myself physically sick and then return to work. Most of my pregnancy seemed to be spent in tears, but they were hidden; to everyone else I was a hard working, pregnant mother who coped well. In the early evenings I'd lie across the bed with a basin below me. One evening, having finished work as usual at 3pm, picked up the boys from school at 3.15 and driven home, I went straight for the bedroom and Robbie followed me through, put his arm around me and said, 'it's a pity you couldn't just lay an egg!' I hadn't realised how much they picked up on. Perhaps everyone was aware and just unable to offer help. It was also strange to be shown sympathy; it had become alien to me. One evening I was crying in the bedroom when the boys came in, I tried to hide my tears but they noticed: just then, the telephone rang and Rory answered. It was Andy's boss, 'he's not in', said Rory, 'and Ken', he said, 'my Mummy's crying'. Robbie hit him on the shoulder as he passed the phone to me. I babbled something about a bad day at work and how I was just a bit down, nothing to worry about. He seemed embarrassed and passed me to his wife who was very kind. My childhood had taught me to be independent and I always found it difficult to ask for help, I felt isolated, I expected people to notice this and offer help but even if they had, perhaps I would have refused.

Then Heather, at three months old was admitted to hospital with broncholitis. There was an epidemic and the wards were full; she took a turn for the worse and was put on a drip. I slept beside her on a z-bed though sleep was almost impossible. It seemed strange that I was coping so well with her in the hospital when I remembered how I had been when Robbie was first admitted. With Heather, I seemed numb to any emotion. She recovered quickly and came home before the end of the week.

Andy and I hardly spoke now, and if we did it was to row. I'd told him I had feelings for someone at work: these emotions had come as a shock and I wasn't sure how to deal with them. I thought speaking to him might help but it only made things worse, because he told me it didn't matter as he was in love with another woman. Whether it was true or just a response to my revelation, I don't know. Neither of us were able to deal with all the upheaval in our lives. His own childhood traumas had been dredged up with the adoption process, so like me, he was questioning many things about us and our lives together.

I was slowly falling apart but I didn't realise what was going on and I didn't want to deal with it. I wanted to show that I could cope with work and children but the emotion of a late, unexpected baby, tied up with all the other emotion of childbirth was taking its toll. So after a horrible row which had upset the boys, I told Andy I wanted a divorce. He didn't disagree, though angry, he went straight to the boys and told them, then left for work.

His initial reaction of anger changed to one of relief. I felt a great weight had been taken from me. The next weeks were terrible; after distressing reactions to our news from family and friends we agreed to remain together, but our hearts weren't in it and after three months the decision was taken that we should separate. This time we told the boys together and they took it easier. We agreed to try and make it as painless as possible for them.

21

Swimming against the tide

When I left Andy, I had been given the rent of a small cottage not far from where we'd been staying. It was a three-bedroom, single storey cottage which sat by itself next to the river Earn. There was a small coppice wood behind it and a farmhouse further down the road was our only neighbour. The inside had been neglected and required a lot of work. I would go in the evenings to clean and paint, I wanted to move in quickly, so after work I'd spend most evenings there. I painted every skirting board and door and emulsioned most of the rooms. Here I was making another cottage habitable with yet more hours of decoration and cleaning. At least this one had a telephone point. I had saved £1,000 and wanted to use it to buy new carpets, I didn't want to risk second-hand carpets because of Robbie's asthma. However, once that was spent, I was counting the pennies. I saw an advert in the local paper selling household goods. The couple were emigrating and therefore selling off everything. I bought a stool, sweeping brush, 2-ring Baby Belling cooker and various crockery items. That evening a friend arrived with more crockery and a set of cooking pans. The cooker had a small oven but all I needed was the top rings for my pressure cooker. I was never able to use convenience foods because of Robbie's allergies to additives, dairy produce and various other foods, so I had to cook fresh meat and vegetables every night. Without a pressure cooker my life would have been impossible. Finally, I went to the local Homebase and bought a pine kitchen table and bench for £25 and my new home was complete.

I hired a van and moved out in the middle of September. Nobody thought it was a good idea and so I didn't feel I could ask any of my friends to help with the move. As I reversed out the drive of the marital home for the last time, there was a sudden bang, I looked out the van window and realised I'd hit my soon to be, ex-husbands car. Quite to the contrary, this was not intentional and after 11 years of marriage, he also realised it wasn't, so nothing was said and I guess he was just glad to see me go. I didn't ask how much damage had been done; I took the shake of his head and the wave of his hand as a sign – a 'get out of my life' sign.

I was finally away and had my own place, yet nothing seemed to change: I didn't feel any better and each day I would cry at some point. I'd done so since I was pregnant and because life was too busy, I hadn't worried too much about it, just putting it down to an extreme case of baby blues. I presumed that once I moved and settled myself in, everything would get better. Friends told me I was suffering from Post Natal Depression, but if I was, it wasn't the reason I left, and I certainly didn't want to acknowledge it.

We had only been in the new house a couple of weeks when winter arrived early. This was bad news, as there was no heating other than a coal fire in the sitting room. Coming in from work and having to light the fire was something I could have done without. My income had taken a plunge as I had given up working for the client that I'd fallen for. He hadn't been helpful and made things difficult. A few months previous he'd refused to increase my hourly rate from £5 to £6 per hour saying he couldn't afford it, but when training his new secretary, I discovered he was paying her £8 per hour. I was furious and made sure he knew it. He, like everyone else was against me leaving Andy, probably because he felt some kind of responsibility, perhaps he thought I'd go back if he made life difficult and made it clear that we would not be a couple. I would never know.

On the days I had no work I went walks with the baby buggy and collected small sticks for the fire as coal was expensive. I felt sure more work would come in: it hadn't been that long since I'd been turning away work. Andy had now moved out of the house as well as leaving his job so he wasn't in a position to give me any money. I forced myself to ring around occasional clients to say I was looking for work. We'll get in touch they would say but I didn't hear anything further. When I'd been busy a couple of other farm secretaries had offered me work that I couldn't fit in, so I rang them now but likewise, they no longer had spare work. As the saying goes, what goes around comes around, and I suppose people felt I was getting my comeuppance. Lots of these old clichéd sayings came to mind, fair weather friends for instance – and I also discovered another one; 'foul weather friends'. These were people I'd never considered close friends who now turned up with wine and flowers to check on me. I discovered that this wasn't out of friendship but was to obtain good gossip. They could confirm how badly I was doing and take away something to talk about at their next dinner party; relieved that things were bad and not good. Bits and pieces came back through the grapevine and I discovered I was present at many dinner parties in the area, but in conversation only. After one such visit, I believed I now had a friend to confide in and told her details of the emotional relationship I'd been tangled in. The next time we spoke on the phone, she blurted out, 'have you seen Fatal Attraction, because I think you need professional help?' I was shocked and distraught; perhaps I really was going mad.

I hadn't seen the film but had heard about it. I hired the video and watched it. To my great relief, it bore little resemblance to my situation. Then a few weeks later, I saw the film, *Dangerous Liaisons,* and was traumatised because it seemed so relevant to what I had gone through. In the end, I probably did need professional help but finding the right kind would have been difficult and many who have asked for it, find themselves worse off. My saviour was books. I borrowed many self-help books from the local library but the writer who had the greatest impact, was Rebecca West. I was stunned by her vision and her sense of justice. Her writings, in many ways, saved me. I also began to understand my own failings where friendship was concerned. Too often, when things were going well, I'd neglected good friends, only to then contact them for support when things went wrong. I'd rarely been there to support and hear about their problems, several eventually gave up on me and as I grew to reflect on these times, I understood why.

My regular clients went out of their way to help find extra work for me; I was humbled by their efforts on my behalf. I also had friends that watched me going off the rails, becoming irrational and falling apart but who stood by me with little comment - they were just there. There were people I thought would have walked away but didn't; one lady, I knew through the Asthma Society turned up one night and handed me a cheque for £75. She said she was a member of a church group which helped families under stress. It was a powerful moment, a real light when there seemed to be none. I offered a coffee but she just handed me the envelope with the explanation and then left. Another client arranged for me to receive sub-contracting work from an accountant he knew who lived nearby. The accountant would drop off a set of accounts to the house and I would work in the evenings when the children were sleeping, in this way, I didn't have to find childminding money. I worked through the night until 3am then without undressing go to bed before getting up with Heather at 6am. I'd catch up with sleep during the day when Heather was having her naps. This job worked well and brought me in much needed cash. Unfortunately, it ended just after I pointed out that their spreadsheets were set up incorrectly and their client VAT claims were short. Two different people rang me to say I was wrong, but after going through the detail, they accepted I was right and then sadly the work stopped. I never heard any further.

Nights were the worst, I would lie awake crying in despair, sometimes frightened by late night calls when no one spoke and then the receiver was replaced. On one occasion a male voice whispered 'I am watching you'. I sat up all night petrified. The main A9 was about a mile from the house and I would look out the windows towards the car headlights and imagine someone was out there watching me.

It was the kids that kept me going as I had to get up to make breakfast and take the boys to school each day. It would be nice to think it was the commitment to my children which drove me on, though I think it was probably the fear of failure, not wanting to admit I could not cope - letting the vultures win. That year a frost settled in the ground in early October and remained until March, no plough saw the ground that winter. A friend brought me a couple of electric, oil-filled radiators, but they were too expensive to use. Instead, we used hot water bottles and slept with our clothes in the beds beside us. This meant they were warm for the morning. However, damp crept everywhere. Books kept me going, every week I'd go to the Auchterarder library and take out another couple. Every so often I'd be taken up short when I read about the way women behaved in society; recognising my own issues or those of others I'd worked with or knew. I began to constantly analyse myself and my actions.

However, the crying didn't stop, it was now February and it began to snow. It snowed continuously and heavily for a couple of days and became deeper than it had been for years. Perthshire is beautiful, the snow added to its beauty, the cold detracted from it. As it became obvious the snow was going to cause travel problems, I left work early and picked up the boys from school and my daughter from her childminder. Then as I approached the main roundabout leading onto the A9 dual carriageway west to Glasgow, the police stopped me. The road was blocked and no cars were to go any further. I explained I lived four miles further along and surely it couldn't be blocked there? No luck, it seemed there were several lorries and many cars blocking the carriageway about ten miles further on and they didn't want to risk it. I didn't want to try and find somewhere for us to stay the night, so drove another route. This time there were no police and no road blocks, though it was clearly going to be closed soon, just by the depth of the snow. The junction joined the dual carriageway a couple of miles further South and I was the only car on the A9. I drove slowly along a whiteout road with only one of the carriageways driveable; it was surreal. I only had to drive for about a mile before I turned off towards home, but I could see lorries parked up further along. I made it home and met my neighbour on her way out and suggested she didn't attempt heading for Glasgow but she decided to risk it. Later I discovered she'd had to spend three nights in a village hall five miles South. It would be three days before she got home. We were lucky and pleased to be home. However, that night the power went off. As we were living hand to mouth, by the second night we had no food. Luckily, I had spare keys to my neighbour's house, so had no choice but to raid their cupboards and borrow bread, sausages and beans. We cooked them in a small pan, which we sat on the coal fire. The kids loved it, I longed for electricity and clear roads.

The Council workers were trying to clear the roads but the snow was relentless. My cottage sat next to a river and about every fifteen minutes a council lorry would arrive with a truck load of snow to dump in the river. It seemed endless.

On the third day, sunshine and clear roads arrived. So did a warm wind and a high tide. The temperature jumped 10 degrees overnight: The snow melted and most of it went quickly into the river in front of my house. This river, which we spent the summer enjoying as a quiet flowing, shallow meander, was now a raging torrent. Perth was badly flooded and I was convinced I was going to be too. My Landlord laughed – the cottage has never been flooded, but he appeased my concerns by begrudgingly delivering a few sandbags and laying them across the road between me and the river. I stayed up all night, going out to check the water level every so often with a small torch and listening to the news for updates. Large round bales of straw raced past as though they were peanuts. Whole tree trunks would swivel down the river without a fight and I stood in the dark drizzle mesmerised, most of all by the noise: My quiet spot was now filled with the roaring of water. It lapped at my feet and the wind almost blew me over, I thought, I could go now and it would appear to be an accident, the children would get my insurance money and have a better life. I wouldn't continue to let everyone down…I stepped closer, feeling the water seep through my shoes and the wind pulling at my hair and jacket. I was on the edge, but I couldn't take the final step, I drew back and went back inside the house; sat beside the remains of the fire and considered my state of mind.

We weren't flooded; I telephoned all my family and friends to reassure them that we had been reprieved.

My own family lived in England and the flooding of Perth was only briefly mentioned on the news, so they were relying on me keeping them informed. I told them the worst was over and I began to put the furniture back on the floor again.

The next night, I was about to turn off the TV and go to bed when a news flash came on the screen: a flood warning for the river Earn. I lifted the torch and went out to see what was happening. The river had risen a little. I decided to wait up a bit longer, and then a neighbour telephoned to check on me. I said I was OK, reassuring him that I would call if things changed. The river became louder and seemed to be rising much faster than the previous night. I had no choice but to remain awake and keep checking. Once again, I went down my path with a torch every twenty minutes only to see the river engulf another riverbank bush and then the little 'Private Fishing' sign on the opposite bank, which had been my marker on the previous night, began to disappear.

Half an hour later when I went to check the river level, my path had several inches of water on it. I ran up the steps and onto the road – but it was dry. How could that be? Where was the water coming from? I swung the torch around until I saw the field next to my house: there was no field, it was all water. I ran along the path to the small road bridge and saw where the water had burst the riverbank and crossed into the field beside me. Breathlessly back at the house, I rang the neighbour who lived about a mile away. I couldn't wake him so rang my Landlord. 'I'm going to be flooded, the water is over the path', I still don't think he believed me but he said he would get help. When I opened my back door again, the water had risen about a foot and was now lapping at my top step. I woke the children. Robbie took fright and immediately had an asthma attack. I plugged in his nebuliser and tried to calm him before I roused Rory who just wanted to sleep. I lifted Heather from her cot and passed her through the living room window to Dave, the farm grieve, who had now arrived by tractor. We tried to lift the carpets, but no sooner were we on our knees rolling them, than the water surged through the floor boards and lifted everything. I unplugged the nebuliser and carried Robbie out and up the path to dry land, the water reached my knees. Dave carried Rory behind me. I then jumped into my car and drove to another neighbour's house peeping my horn to wake them as the water was heading in their direction but nobody appeared to be there. If they were, at least they had an upper floor.

My Landlord put us up for the night. We were a sorry looking bunch standing on the doorstep of his mansion: me, soaked and bedraggled with a baby in my arm and two young exhausted children in their pyjamas. He took pity and showed us to a set of lovely rooms and also gave us separate bathrooms which the boys were very impressed by.

In the morning I went down and saw my house standing in a huge basin of water, a large panda toy which I had put out for the bin collection was floating around upside down in about two feet of water. Several people stood around looking; the tractor men from the farm had been working on the road digging a ditch across to the river which had now dropped, to try and release the water. One wore large waders and he offered to take me into the house. I jumped on his back and he carried me through the water to the back door - the site which greeted me was devastating - I hadn't thought about the mud the leaves and the muck. About six inches of muddy, smelly water was throughout the house. My new lino, which I had taken a great deal of time choosing, was warped and floating. I wasn't prepared for this. It was a strange sight - the only piece of dry land near my house was the small area where we had laid the sandbags.

When I'd moved in, I'd decided to wait a few months before arranging house insurance. I had had insurance for twelve years after all and never required it, a few months without wouldn't be a problem or so I thought. It was one of the costliest mistakes I could have made. The Estate owner said we could stay as long as required, but I didn't want to impose and knew I'd be on edge in case the children broke or damaged anything valuable. Instead, I telephoned Andy and the next day we moved in with him. I only lasted a week, it wasn't a good week, very strained. I went to the house every night and tried to clean up: a friend helped me to wash the mud from the floors. I kept the coal fire lit and borrowed paraffin and gas heaters to try and dry the place. Then someone said that they make things worse by creating moisture. A local builder gave me a loan of a dehumidifier which seemed to make a difference. One evening, on arriving back at Andy's, I had been crying on the way home, as I went in to the house he looked over and said scathingly, 'what's wrong with you?' 'What the hell do you think is wrong with me?' I screamed, and left the room. The next weekend the floorboards were dry enough to lay carpets - they had been hung in the boiler room of the Mansion House to dry. We moved back in. If there had been any hope of me recovering from the depression, it was now gone. I became more depressed: frequently thinking of suicide. I would drive the car too fast around a corner which I had chosen and be sure not to have my seat belt on. I had had so many car accidents in the past that no-one would realise I had meant it this time. I suppose the only thing that stopped me was the fear I might not actually die, only be badly injured. I couldn't afford to be ill - only dead. If I heard that someone had been killed in an accident I felt angry - someone who wanted to live being killed whilst I wanted to die and was still here. I found a solicitor and made out a will then took out extra life insurance.

It was a constant fight with myself. I would wake on some days, determined not to give in to the depression.

One morning on seeing my face in the mirror, I was so shocked at how bad I looked, I remembered the lady in the hospital who'd been brought to despair by her husband, and thought I had to sort myself out, as no one else was going to do it for me. I bathed and put on make up for the first time in weeks, and then I telephoned the Bank Manager to make an appointment. The next day, I found a bright and tidy outfit; I took time over my hair and tied a bright scarf through it. With plenty of makeup, I thought I didn't look too bad. When I saw the bank manager I told him how well my business was doing and I now needed to change my car: I asked for a loan of £5,000. He seemed happy with this and after some discussion I obtained very good terms. He then asked if I had any collateral, which of course I didn't. This seemed to worry him a little but I offered my life insurance - suggesting he could always come and shoot me if I didn't pay. I left with the loan agreed and felt I now had no choice, with extra payments going out monthly I would have no time to feel sorry for myself, I would have to work very hard to keep up repayments. I would buy the smartest car I could find and let people think I was doing well. Maybe then I would get extra work: I believed I knew the psychology of people when it came to business. I was going to make a new image for myself, I would fit in if I had to. After several discussions and almost buying a BMW, I went for the Astra, but not just an ordinary model; it had to be an up-market model. I found the car I wanted, and it was red.

I started to apply for steady jobs in Perth as my financial situation was now desperate; I also opened a new credit card. Then after being in the house for three weeks, black mould began to appear on several of the walls. I telephoned the Landlord and a joiner arrived – 'you'll need to move out', he said, 'the whole house will have to be stripped and dried out properly'. That evening I thought I could never cope with another day.

Somehow I pulled myself together again with the help of friends and family who were always at the end of the telephone. There was another empty cottage on the same Estate so I rang to ask if I could rent it while mine was being dried out. There was a long pause, I said 'please', excuses were being given and I felt myself get on my knees, phone in hand and then I pleaded with the last bit of energy and pride I had, 'please can I get the house, I have nowhere else to go'. He gave in, the rent was a little extra but I still had a home.

They thought it would take about three months for the work to be complete - so once again I was moving house only four months after my last move and that promise I'd made to myself never to move again. I was now buying food on my credit cards, the boys needed trousers and I bought them from charity shops to their groans. However, work was beginning to pick up and my sister lent me £300 when things became desperate. My other sister came to stay for a week and look after the children while I attended a stall at the Royal Agricultural Show. It was during this week that I first saw the internet in action. I was amazed by the technology and keen to know more.

After several months, and still not returning to my house, I wanted a break: I organised a visit to my mums for a week in the summer holidays, a few days away from everything could do no harm, so we set off for Nottingham. 'HAZEL, HAZEL!' my sister, Yvette, screamed up the stairs. I could tell by her voice that something was wrong and ran towards her as she shouted 'Your car is gone'. I knew she was mistaken, she just wasn't seeing it. I walked to the window and looked down to an empty space where my car was recently parked. Lifting the telephone I asked if I should dial 999 - YES said Yvette. It was the second night of our holiday, visiting my mother and now the break from all the stress of the last year was turning into a further disaster. The police took the details but were not greatly interested. They had heard it all too often before: It seemed that Nottingham was the car theft capital of the UK.

The next morning the Police rang back, 'we've found your car', they said. 'It's been used to ram raid various pubs overnight, so we have to fingerprint it, but you can pick it up tomorrow'. The next day was spent arranging to uplift the car and the baby seat which had somehow ended up in a different police station. 'Can you describe the baby seat?' asked the charming looking policeman, 'well, it's got navy stripes and when last seen had a black jelly baby stuck to it!' 'That'll do for me' he smiled.

The rear windscreen had been smashed and I had to replace it before travelling home. The police said I would be able to drive it, but first they had to show me how to hot wire the ignition in order to start it – the ignition lock had been removed. Then, it was agreed the best place for it to be left for the rest of my holiday was the police station, as it was likely it would just get stolen again if I parked it anywhere in Nottingham. So, that was my lovely new car; being driven home with wires hanging out the steering wheel, having been bashed at the rear end and with knife cuts throughout the interior. Somehow it was the knife cuts which upset me most: they were so pointless. Half way up the motorway, the driver's electric mirror went on fire and I had to pull on to the hard shoulder to put it out. Soon, after I arrived home, my eldest sister came for a visit with her fiancé – he gave me a hug 'you'd have a nervous breakdown, but you can't fit in, can you?' He smiled. Little things counted for so much then.

22

Under moral panic

One of the most significant changes which I was unprepared for was my new status of 'single mother' and the expectations and baggage which came with it...baggage which I had not packed and did not want. Unlike the luggage which disappears at airports, it sticks close by, refuses to get lost and often trips you up when you're not looking. The problem was made much worse a few weeks after I separated: The current Prime Minister of the Tory government, John Major, began his 'Back to Basics' campaign and every newspaper carried headlines of scrounging single mothers abusing the benefits system and producing delinquent children. There was even a Panorama program about it. What was later to become known as the 'Moral Panic' of 1993, saw the 'traditional family' as best and single mothers as a scourge on society. I took it personally; felt they were aiming at me, and yet I didn't claim benefits and was determined that I never would. The disgust I felt years later when I heard the truth about John Major and his affair with Edwina Currie, only matched that which I felt for Margaret Thatcher.

When making arrangements for our separation, Andy had announced he wanted to keep the boys. I was distraught and rang my mother. She said 'agree to it, there is no way he'll keep and look after the boys on his own, he's trying to blackmail you'. She was right. I agreed and on the day before the move, he said that perhaps he wasn't organised enough to keep them, I should take them until he managed to arrange suitable childcare. He'd collect them in a couple of weeks. We explained this to the boys but as my mother had so rightly guessed, he never did bring up the subject again. Unfortunately, neither of us ever explained the change of decision to the boys. Five years later, my youngest son informed me that he didn't realise he was leaving his father for good. He thought it was just for a couple of weeks and had been forever waiting on his father's arrival to collect him. This was only one of the traumas caused, no matter how much you want to protect your children from the upset of divorce, it is like pretending you can cut yourself without leaving a scar.

Another unexpected outcome of separating was the response from other people: Some friends that we'd seen often when a couple, now completely cut me off. Perhaps they thought if they left us alone and offered no help, we would 'come to your senses'. Others become anxious, not because our marriage had fallen apart, but because, if it could happen to us, it may also happen to them.

Some women friends were not allowed to visit me on their own – in case I fed them with wrong ideas. I had become a bad influence. Other women offered their husband's services – to put up curtains or hammer in nails. However, I had to be on my guard for women who wanted to dump their husbands on me. They would usually be planning their own escape, so would helpfully offer their partner in the hope that I was a suitable alternative.

Because of these unforeseen problems, it became essential to work out for myself what kind of future relationship, if any, I wanted. However, this changed on an hourly, daily, weekly and annual basis. One of my definite 'no goes' was that I would not get involved with any married men. Then, because of the earlier bad experience – I decided work colleagues were also off limits. This reduced the possibility of me meeting someone; however, on reflection by sticking to these two rules, with great difficulty on some occasions, they were the right ones. I never lost my self-respect and can look back with no regrets. I had to remind myself that despite believing I could think clearly, my brain was probably mashed potato.

I thought I would be a good single mum; one that is reasonable, lets the children see their father and doesn't expect money for herself, just the kids. I was not going to be one of John Major's scroungers. I watched the Panorama programme about women who intentionally got pregnant in order to get a house. There was a lot of debate and arguments over the reasons and rights of such a system. As I wearily hung baby clothes around the house to dry and fought my exhaustion, I couldn't understand why these great minds weren'y asking, what to me, was the vital question: In a civilized, wealthy society, why is it necessary for a woman to get herself pregnant in order to have a house?

In my mind, such a ploy was no worse than women who married in order to have a house, money or social life.

A great many hypocrisies in our society were revealed to me during this time. Being a Farm Secretary, it was a major part of my job to lodge claims for farming subsidies. Tens of thousands of pounds were being paid from taxpayers' money to already wealthy farmers, for no apparent reason other than they happened to have a farm. The new IACS system was introduced and subsidy levels, already high were being increased hugely. These were genuine schemes, which anyone in their situation would have been entitled to claim on. However, this type of subsidy was seen as honourable, a competitive hysteria gathered over who could claim the most; who's subsidy cheques reached six figures. The historical need for such subsidies was gone, no one in our country was starving and over production certainly was not helping those starving elsewhere. It seemed strange, that although I was not relying on the state for direct support; instead, I was being supported in an indirect way by cattle and sheep subsidies and I couldn't see why one was worse than the other. A few farmers did equate this money with social security benefits, but most were oblivious. One client was in trouble with their bank and I was asked to help. They had clearly overspent on their business overdraft for many years, taking expensive holidays and spending excessively on their house. The bank had froze their overdraft and they were struggling to get by. The farmer's wife complained that she had to buy a new washing machine on HP. 'I'm so ashamed', she said. 'I've never had to borrow to buy goods before'. I was speechless. I couldn't point out that a business overdraft was borrowed money, just as an HP loan was. It just happened that one was more expensive than the other.

* * * *

It was during these early days on my own, that I discovered true loneliness, especially when the kids were ill or there was a problem at school and there was no one to share the burden and worries with: no one to ask advice on whether I should call a doctor in the middle of the night or speak to a headmaster about teacher problems. However, I also accepted that these were short spells of loneliness in comparison to the solitude experienced when I shared a bed with someone to whom all emotional connection was lost.

After eighteen months I did try to get medical help but I think the doctor suffered from a different fear - what if this woman isn't capable of looking after her children? And instead of treating me, he convinced me that he was more depressed than I was and asked for help in sourcing a relaxation tape he used to own. The visit also confirmed my original suspicions about the system: two days later, 'out of the blue' the Health Visitor arrived on my doorstep to check how things were. I had never seen her before yet she said she 'was just passing' and thought she'd call in and see how we were. Luckily, I had friends visiting at the time and the children and I were in a good state of happiness, so we didn't see her again. It didn't make me feel comfortable though, so I thought it best not to discuss my depression with the doctor again.

I realised, for the sake of my children I had to survive in order to be of any use to them. Although there were the dark times when the alternative seemed to be the more suitable and kinder option, most of the time, I wanted to survive and make sure I was there for my kids. I tried hard not let the children see me depressed. I managed to act on automatic pilot during the day; feeding, changing, cleaning and playing with them and then at night, once they were in bed, I would break down. Cry for several hours, pull myself together, do some late evening accounts work, or writing and sleep in between my daughter's night feeds. Unbelievably, this worked, as years later when the boys were teenagers, I discussed this period of depression with them and asked how they had felt about it? The boys were amazed and only remembered the times as being mainly fun: gathering kindling, long walks and swing parks, the only bad bit being the cold and that I seemed to spend a lot of time on my computer in the office.

The next priority was to keep the house. I had been given it from a client but despite many peoples' assumptions, I paid full rent. It was important to pay this on time and not lose our home. Then there was food. We could do without treats but needed a reasonable diet. Having been a student for two years, I was adept at eating on a pittance, macaroni, lots of potatoes and rice and I would go to our local Safeway late on Sunday evenings where I would find chicken and meat at much reduced prices.

Within two months, Andy announced he was in love and was going to get married. The children went to visit and came home excited and happy, they had a lovely day and Miss X was wonderful – played games, bought them sweets and told jokes. I failed to contain my emotion and burst into tears, and then stupidly asked 'is she better than me?' (It seemed a reasonable assumption at this point.) The boys look shocked and suddenly so was I and to make matters worse, I knew I'd just ruined their nice day. They cried and we had a long talk that night about why Mums were so daft.

A single mother is very vulnerable. It is frightening to think of the responsibility that lies on your shoulders. In desperation, I was prepared to put faith in people I would not look twice at ten years down the road. I craved a sex life and unbeknown to me, this freely imparts itself to others, yet they failed to notice the bit that says 'NOT WITH YOU'. A friend told me to forget about men, just use them for money, and perhaps this had to be an option. I flirted a bit in order to get work, not serious flirting as always I knew there was a line I couldn't cross. I knew I could look quite attractive when dressed well but also believed I'd create horror if anyone discovered the scars below the clothes. It could be a dangerous line, but never felt particularly guilty about using my female wiles to obtain work: my work was good and I earned the money appropriately. I asked one friend who had a continual stream of male friends how she did it. 'It's in the eyes', she said. 'Use your eyes'. I thought I would give this a go, so when working at a new training job some distance away, the factor asked to see me about the management reports. I thought it was a good opportunity to try out the 'eye' technique and looked him directly in the eyes and held my stare. It worked; he changed immediately towards me but became uncomfortable. I was a bit shocked and carried on discussing the reports. The following week, I received a call from the secretary asking if I would visit to do an extra day's training. I was delighted - a bit of extra work. On the day of the training, we had no sooner begun working when the secretary made a point of telling me that the factor was very happily married to his second wife and had young children. I cringed. I only used the eye technique on one more occasion, the businessman, not a farmer, rang me in the evening to ask if I'd meet him for dinner to discuss the software further. I was under no illusion about the invite and I quite liked the man, but I thought I should check with a friend before I allowed the situation to go any further. My friend told me he was married with three children. I was annoyed at myself, I had to sort things: I rang a male sales colleague and asked him to join us at the dinner, and then intentionally arrived late. I survived the evening being glared at across a frosty dinner table. He of course didn't buy the software and I lost out on the training. I decided that this 'eye' technique was too risky and implied more that I was prepared to give so that was the end of it.

Many people thought I was courageous. I never felt courageous: Naïve maybe, stupid perhaps, at an abyss but not courageous. If I had known how hard the early years were to be, I would probably never have made the move and instead accepted the life I'd chosen. Following through on the old adage that 'I'd made my bed, so I should lie in it'. Then again who can say: Perhaps not.

When we were children, I must have been about twelve, my mother arranged our one and only holiday so it is easy to recollect. She booked a small hotel in the seaside town of Ayr, about 20 miles from our village. Not far in today's travelling distances but it seemed as though we were going on a great adventure at the time. We were excited when we heard we were going to be staying in an hotel. I imagined it would be like the one in our village, large windows, waiters and bars. But when we arrived it was only a house, a big stone house but still a house. Mum had booked only one room for herself and the five of us. It was a large room with bay windows but it was old and slightly fusty. On the weekend before the holiday, she had her holiday pay, £200, stolen by a pick-pocket in Glasgow Central Station. Mum was distraught that evening. After a couple of 'phone calls, she walked to the top of our street to visit a man she only knew slightly but was retired and quite well off. He lent her £50, which was just enough to pay for the room. We went on the holiday and spent the week on the beach. There were no ice cream treats or buckets and spades but luckily it was nice weather. On leaving the hotel, Mum organised the five of us to stand on the step with the luggage and then went back inside. I followed her and from a short distance watched as she asked the owner if he could give her 50p for a taxi to take us to the station. I can still feel her shame and how she cringed as he stood unmoved and refused her any help. I thought I would never put myself in that position.

It was also during this holiday that I discovered

how vile newspaper reporters could be: An elderly lady staying at the hotel won a great deal of money on a horse bet. The newspaper reporter arrived to interview her. She was very nervous about being interviewed and asked my Mum to stay with her during the interview. I was also allowed to be there. As she showed the young male reporter into her room, she apologised for the ladder in her tights, joking she had all these thousands yet torn tights. The reporter brushed it off and then sat with her for at least half an hour asking about her background and what she intended doing with the money. She had a family, grandchildren and told of various hardships in her life. Finally, he took a photograph and left. The next day there was a huge picture in the front of the paper with the headline: 'Thousands of Pounds in the bank but only one pair of laddered tights'. The poor lady was distraught and would speak to no one before leaving for home.

I had read that during a time of family turmoil it is important to keep as much consistency in the children's lives as possible. I therefore thought it would be best if I could keep the children at the same school, despite it being further away and requiring me to drive them there and back each day. I also decided that every Sunday we would get into a routine of having breakfast, going into a nearby village to buy a paper and then visiting the swing park. We did this for many months. I read the papers, in small bouts, interspersed by fallouts, 'watch this mum' and occasional bumps as they played on the swings and chutes.

Human nature is strange. People can be overwhelmingly helpful and generous in a crisis but equally mean and spiteful. As if afraid that someone's misery might allow them too much generosity or that too much sympathy isn't good for a person. It's as though they are saying 'bad things happen to you, because you are a bad person'. I even bought into this belief myself for a while. I was on my own with children through my own choice and therefore deserved to be flooded. I wasn't the only one flooded; a great swathe of Perth had also been flooded. Funds were set up to help the flood victims that didn't have insurance. Some spoke openly of how the help fund was being abused by people wanting new kitchen electrics, carpets etc. Maybe there were some people who found a way of doing this, I only know that I had to sit for hours in a portacabin with the kids, and then was subjected to a detailed interview by a stranger who then decided how deserving a cause I was. It felt humiliating. I received two new mattresses, a fridge freezer and electricity stamps. These are the kind of moments that I only subjected myself to because I was a mother – these are truly unselfish moments when I knew I would rather starve than ask for help but I put my children first.

When I went back the second time to ask for more electricity stamps, the lady who made the decisions looked at my notes and then me. She mentioned my work and then looked at my smart appearance and I knew what she was thinking that the same thing the Business Grant Officer had said to me, when I applied for a small business loan: 'you work for some of the wealthiest land owners in this county, yet you want us to give you help. Why can't you just ask them?' I never returned. My credit card balance continued to rise.

It was to take four months to repair my house so I decided I wouldn't bother unpacking. We would make do with living out of boxes. The four months turned into nine months and I'm afraid that whole period of time is almost a blank to me. When I wasn't working, I was sleeping. The children were neglected. I believe they must have been although I cannot remember. Of those nine months waiting on my house being repaired, I only have memories for about half a dozen days.

The cottage was part of a group of three houses and we had what seemed, a nice family next door with a teenage daughter and a younger girl. I let the older girl come into the house, gave her a few clothes that I no longer wore and was happy for her to play with the kids. But she stole money from us, then my house key and finally I had to call the police with her parents agreement – she had done such things before and they didn't know how to stop her.

I lost my daughter. She was only two and a half at the time and I was completely frantic, running around the farm buildings, up and down the house stairs, not knowing which way to turn. Then I saw a man walk up the long driveway with her in his arms. She had tried to follow the boys, who had gone to visit a friend. She crossed the road as a tractor came. When walking on country roads with her, I had taught her to sit down on the verge as soon as we heard a vehicle; this was the safest way if I had the boys and a bag. I'd know she was in one place and not likely to run out on the road. So when she'd heard the tractor coming, she just sat down in the middle of the road. Thank goodness it hadn't been a car and thank goodness he didn't report what had happened.

Once again, I contemplated my own death, but then I began to consider the possibility of an afterlife - what would happen if there was another life and you could still feel all the emotions you felt in this life? How awful – I could kill myself only to then discover that I was awake elsewhere and have to suffer the agony of watching my family without being able to help them. I suppose at the end of the day that was what stopped me most of all – there was no guarantee that when I died, I would be truly dead.

One of my most important clients was a financial software company from England. I had won the contract to do all their training in Scotland and I knew in the long term this would prove lucrative work; however, I had to build up my relationship with them as they built up their client base. I always made sure I was very professional when dealing with them. It was important they thought I was busy and in demand rather than desperate for work. I certainly didn't want to let them know about my home circumstances. One day as I sat with the kids watching TV, the phone rang, it was this Company's Office Manager. She asked if I had time to speak with the Director. 'Yes', I said, 'but can you hold for a minute?' I placed the receiver next to the phone and then lifted Heather and ran up stairs to put her in her cot in case she began to cry. I then sped back down the stairs. Out of puff, I lifted the receiver, put my hand over my mouth and breathed in and out quickly and loudly to try and get my breath back. Then I said 'Hello Mandy, you can put me through now'. She sounded a bit strange and asked if I was alright. I said yes and then was put through to the Director and the call passed without further incident. However, on replacing the receiver, I anguished over Mandy's reaction, then to my horror, I realised that I should have put my hand over the receiver and not my mouth: she would have heard my heavy puffing and then sudden change of tone when I spoke. The incident didn't cause any problems between me and the company but some time later when they discovered I'd been flooded they seemed shocked that I hadn't mentioned it and I think things fell into place for Mandy.

A secretary at an Estate where I'd trained, asked me to lunch one day and we became friends. When it was time to move back into my house, Janice offered to help and I gratefully accepted. She arrived in her Ford Fiesta to help but was rather horrified at my lack of organisation and stormed around the house throwing things into boxes and trying to get me to sort things. She filled her car and drove between the houses moving the boxes and furniture until we were left with the three piece suite. I said I'd hire a van for it, but she was adamant that it would fit in the back of the fiesta and somehow it did one piece at a time, with the back door open. She drove my entire contents to the refurbished house and I treated her to a fabulous meal at a local restaurant that evening.

23

Taking the medicine

During this first year, Robbie's asthma had become much worse and continued to deteriorate, then on one of his regular six weekly hospital visits, he told the nurse he wasn't taking his steroid tablets. I was shocked as I reminded him every morning to take them. I argued this with her, but then Robbie admitted that he pretended to take them, and when I wasn't looking, he put them in the bin. I was so taken aback, I sat speechless. The nurse asked to see me alone and Robbie stayed with the consultant. I was given a long lecture on how it was unreasonable of me to expect a ten year old to take his own medicines and that it was my responsibility, not just to tell him to take them but to actually administer them. I didn't really have any argument with that, other than that Robbie had been on medicines all of his life and seemed mature about his condition. A few minutes later the consultant came in and told us that Robbie had told him that the reason he was putting his tablets in the bin was because they tasted so horrible. The consultant had therefore tasted one of the tablets and discovered that they were the foulest tasting things he'd ever had. He then said it was possible to get the same tablets with a coating to mask the taste and that he'd order them in the future, not only for Robbie but for all young patients who required them.

I was left sitting in the small consulting room feeling diminished when a young student doctor came in and started chatting about Robbie's illness and his treatment. During the conversation she said 'why don't you see if you can get him in to Glenalmond School on a bursary or scholarship? My brother went there and they have a nurse on duty 24 hours'. I would never have considered such an option but it seemed like a gift, there would be no harm in making enquiries.

The following week I wrote to Glenalmond; a mixed boarding school nearby and explained my circumstances with Robbie's health problems. I asked if there was any possibility of being given financial assistance. Within a week, we were invited to a meeting with the headmaster, which went well and he was supportive of our position. He asked Robbie if he liked reading, and Robbie replied that he did. 'Good, what book are you reading at present?' Well that was easy as he'd been reading one in the car on the way over, 'Terry Pratchet' he replied. There was silence and the headmaster looked at him with some puzzlement, 'I don't think I know him', he said. 'Well', Robbie said, 'I have all his books', and we gave no further explanation.

We were given a tour of the school and the grounds, which were beautiful, but we then realised we would have to wait another year before Robbie could be admitted as he was still too young. However, I now had the bit between my teeth and I arranged to see if the other local boarding school would give him the opportunity. I made contact and once again was invited to meet the headmaster. It was a good meeting and he said he was happy to put an application forward for a bursary and an assisted place. Robbie would also have to sit an entrance exam, and if he passed then there would be a place for him. He confirmed they had 24 hour nursing facilities and they were willing to take responsibility for his care and medication. Unlike the state school: they had refused to administer his medicines without forms being completed for each bout of illness. Robbie passed the exam and would go as a boarder the following September.

When you're living your life and it is hard, and you're just trying to keep going, swimming against the tide, then you don't see it as exceptional or interesting, it is only on reflection you understand why so many others were interested and wanted to comment. Here I was, a modern woman, 'having it all' in terms of a business and children, but also, I was a single mother who didn't claim benefits and now I had one of my children at a boarding school. The fact that I originated from a council house was the biggest shock to many.

Another human quirk I'd become aware of was that wealthy people didn't like it when someone of a lower social class acquired something valuable or did something, such as a skiing holiday, which was meant to be reserved for their class. It was OK if they gifted the benefit, but for them to rise above their station and do it for themselves caused consternation. I saw this several times; one particular instance happened when a farm secretary I knew purchased a new Mercedes car. Her boss who must have been one of the wealthiest landowners in the country was irritated that his secretary was going to be driving a Mercedes. Another time, a client met his accountant's secretary on a plane: he couldn't get over the fact that she was using expensive luggage, even to the point he rang his accountant and told him he must be paying her too much if she could afford such items. He didn't consider that she may have saved to buy the luggage. 'Perhaps she was left a legacy?' I suggested, trying to alleviate his anxiety.

I suppose I fell into this category of being above 'my station' by sending Robbie to a boarding school. One lady who had two sons at an English boarding school popped in for a coffee out of the blue, she'd never been in my house before. During coffee she kindly informed me that I should be aware that it wasn't only about school fees, it was about all the extra costs involved in such schools and how would I manage to send Robbie on the skiing trips etc? I responded 'I won't send him; he is there to be looked after medically and get an education'. She seemed taken aback by my response, left and didn't return.

I do admit that I was nervous about how he would fit in, but his housemaster put us at ease and Robbie settled quickly and made a few friends. Unfortunately, I made the mistake of inviting one to stay over half term, as he couldn't go to his own home abroad. When he came into the cottage, he couldn't hide his shock at the Baby Belling cooker and our lack of furniture and material goods. Robbie did thrive at the school, went on to become Pipe Major and had some wonderful experiences, not skiing but mountaineering. He also made friends, especially with the ladies who ran the clinic. Most importantly he survived and received a fantastic education. Rory also went to the school but only after his first year at the local comprehensive had turned into a disaster for him, where he was bullied and beaten. By that time, my business had grown substantially: computerised accountings systems were the norm and tighter controls on EU money meant more paperwork. I now employed one lady, but as I didn't want to feel too responsible for other people's lives, I generally gave work out on a contract basis rather than employing more. There was enough money to pay for Rory's education and we even began to afford the occasional holiday: mostly in Belgium to visit my cousin (it was visiting Lynn that I experienced my first flight and obtained my first passport at the age of 33). I never stopped appreciating the ability to choose to go out for a meal without worrying if I could afford to do it.

It took three years and yet another house move for me to recover fully from the depression and for the night crying to stop, but it did. And we stayed in our next house for a full ten years. I no longer needed to flirt to get business, my work spoke for itself. I gave up on the hope of being in a relationship and found support through friends. My painful period of self-analysis had given me a solid foundation to work from. I felt secure in who I was and what I wanted to do with my life although there were traumas yet to come which nothing could prepare me for. I at least understood that I could survive when I thought otherwise. That knowledge would always be with me.

24

The legacy of swans

It was a dreich day when I turned into the road end and began the drive along a memory lane of dirt track and gravel. Not much had improved since I lived here over 30 years ago. After a few minutes drive, I drew to a halt confused; was it straight ahead or do I turn right? There was a new farm building sitting beside the road but then I spotted a familiar shed tucked behind it. I turned the car to the right and saw the house. Smaller than I remembered, yet tidier and more surprisingly, it was lived in. I parked the car. 'This is it', I turned to Robbie beside me who looked fairly unimpressed and was a bit on edge about driving into the grounds of a private estate. I asked if he wanted to come with me to have a look but he didn't. I left him with my partner, Dmytro, who'd come along for the drive and was slightly bemused by my ability to embarrass a 30 year old son, in the way only a mother can. I walked up to the house. There was nobody about, I knocked, half hoping that no one was in. As I waited for a response, I looked around: The old shed where we kept junk and had kept the collie dog, had been renovated to become part of the house. There were ornamental sculptures around the grounds. It was still peaceful, no one answered, not even a dog. I turned towards the old shed where a photograph had been taken on Robbie's Christening day: A large, new Massey Ferguson tractor had framed the back of the picture. I wore my mother's red suit with padded shoulders, cradling my first baby, looking like the girl I was and unaware of the life ahead. I pulled my mobile phone from my pocket and took a picture of the place I'd been before mobile phones existed. The picture, this time was of a spacious, but still crumbling red stone building. Now, instead of protecting old farm machinery, it was filled with sculptures and other artefacts. As I walked back to the car I remembered the day I tried to save the swan and was glad the house had not fallen down, but like me, it had been reconstructed and still had a role to play.

End

An Education

My mother was a catwalk model
before she married,
afterwards, she kept her elegant ways;
wore stiletto shoes with ease.
The gold and silver, six-inch heels
clicked bright sparks along the grey
pavements of my childhood.

I moved to college and won top prize:
Gilt-edged parchment invited families to the ceremony.
My mother arrived well groomed, but shorter:
She'd had to borrow Granny's boots;
flat, fur-lined, tight with zips.

She slipped her feet below plush seats,
hiding the cost of my higher education.